Songs from the House of Pilgrimage

The biography of a mystic and a way of life that foretells

the future of Christianity.

Dr. Stephen Isaac

The Christward Ministry
San Marcos, CA

ISBN-13: 978-0910378444
ISBN-10: 0910378444

Thy statutes have been my songs
in the house of my pilgrimage.
Psalm 119:54

Flower A. Newhouse

CONTENTS

Introduction

I met Flower for the first time when I was ten years old. It was 1935; she was on a speaking tour into the Pacific Northwest and had an engagement in Medford, Oregon, where my family lived. My mother, who had been searching for her true spiritual path, noticed the advertisement in the local newspaper and was prompted to attend the lecture. It was my great good fortune that she took me with her. To this day I can relive that moment which has never dimmed in my memory. The lecture hall was in a downtown building. We were sitting near the front in wooden folding chairs. Suddenly, Flower entered the room. She was dressed in white and walked to a chair, turned and looked at the audience, her face radiant and smiling. I stared at her, scarcely believing my eyes. I was sure I was looking into the eyes of an angel. I remember nothing of what she said that night. My eyes alone stored the deathless impression of this first meeting. I couldn't fathom the significance of the transformation that took place on that occasion, but something changed in my life, and things were never to be the same again. I am told that when I returned home that evening, I said to one of my family, "I saw an angel."

How did this affect my life? Looking back, it was as if I had been asleep and that evening I was awakened by this wondrous being and reminded that it was time to set childish things aside and take up the path once more. I was slow to stir, but the invitation was absolutely irresistible.

I was rather backward in school at this stage of my life,

7

preferring to daydream those hours away rather than settle down to the work at hand. Soon after that fateful meeting, my schoolwork began to improve, and I took an interest in things previously neglected. Though a part of me was still holding back, longing to remain in the sleepy shadows a little longer, gradually the light prevailed and, more and more, I paid heed to every word from Flower that reached our home.

After that, we would see her each year for a lecture visit. These occasions stretched out for a week of meetings in the summertime—called the Medford Hilltop Conclaves, after the name of the ranch where they were held. A small group formed to study the emerging teachings that Flower and her husband, Lawrence, were publishing together. Word came in 1940 that they had at last found the property so long searched for to establish their work—at that time, 440 acres of land with a small stone cottage in the remote hills near Escondido, California. Soon, World War II brought both the need and the opportunity for my family and several others from the Medford area to move to Southern California and join the beginning of Questhaven Retreat.

For myself, it marked the end of occasional reminders of life's purposefulness and the onset of daily endeavor Godward. During the summer of 1943 I was privileged to spend several weeks as a guest in the Questhaven home of Flower and Lawrence, just before entering the U.S. Army. Those memorable days proved to be the most insightful and formative of my life yet. I was to learn what it was like to live in the presence of one whose own consciousness was unbrokenly linked with the Inner Worlds. As the days passed, I listened to her every word and watched her every movement. Her tranquility never fluctuated; her outshining love never lapsed. Nor was there anything about her reminiscent of a façade or of a preoccupation with keeping up appearances. Everything she was flowed from an inward Source unencumbered by guile or ego. The impression this made on me was profound, penetrating to the foundations of my being. After these many years, I can still see her cleaning her kitchen, singing as she alone could sing—joyfully and with a beauty belonging to another world.

It was then I realized that what was hers to do, she did with the same spirit and gladness, whatever it was—housework, caring for her pets, attending Lawrence or her guests, answering letters, preparing a lecture, or speaking to one seeking her counsel. In all these things she was one and the same soul. I was to realize her nature was vastly different from mine, and though she understood the nature of others, hers was true to the Kingdom of her origin. She was indeed an angel among us.

From that point onward, I found my life changing and accelerating. I woke up to the fact of both my lower and higher selves. The necessity to conquer the former was much on my mind after that. A few months later, while serving overseas in England, I received a letter from Flower in which she foresaw for me a career in psychology. Nothing could have been further from my mind—one of those "out of the blue" events that characterize the hand of God turning our lives in new directions. It was to be a rich and rewarding journey.

As the new knowledge grew, adding itself upon the foundation of Christian Mysticism laid in place by Flower, I gradually realized something more. It was not enough simply to acquire knowledge. The more I became aware of Flower's reality, the more I understood that, without application, spiritual knowledge was empty. It never impressed her what I knew about something unless she saw how my life was changed because of it—how I lived my life differently as a result. Reincarnation, karma, the Hierarchy, the great initiations and illumination, the Kingdom of the Angels, the Inner Worlds and, most of all, the reality of the Living Christ—all of these, if they were no more than concepts, missed "the many splendored thing." What counted was that you lived by these truths and that they shaped your destiny. Nothing less sufficed. She was like a gardener whose purpose was to foster growth, and that alone was worthy endeavor.

Though I have failed more times than I can remember, because of her steadfastness, her tireless exampleship, and her fathomless love I have also crossed over thresholds in consciousness, any one of which would make this incarnation marvelously worthwhile.

Of all the lessons I've learned as her pupil, not one matches the value of aspiring toward unbroken spiritual integrity—what the Great Ones call *centeredness*—keeping true to the Presence of God, a Presence that is everywhere, in everything and everyone, always. She exemplifies this in a manner unequaled in my experience. It is synonymous with agape love, and what makes Flower's expression of this love unforgettable is that it flows out of God's World, not out of man's. It is the love that the Lord Christ taught to his disciples, a love that is altogether pure and truthful.

Finally, there was about Flower such a deep imprinting of her life with our Lord Emmanuel, that it rekindled inklings of remembrance in those around her—perhaps the sense of wonder one would have felt in His presence or the thrill of sharing the revelations of the Sermon on the Mount to friends in a distant village. Altogether, there was about Flower the mysterious and unmistakable recreation, awake and alive, of this One who was the greatest of earth-born souls, the Lord Christ. Of all of her gifts that was her finest.

Dr. Stephen Isaac

Prologue

This is a book about a teacher of life—an unforgettable woman whose gift of clairvoyance may stand unequaled in the world and whose lesson to her pupils is always herself living the life and following the way. It is also a story: believable because it has happened and prophetic because it foretells the future of ourselves. The story is about two people, their love for each other and their extraordinary dedication to God.

As the story unfolds, so does the meaning of life: the wisdom teachings, the inner worlds, reincarnation, the disciplines, the initiations and illumination. Life is seen as a school in which the prime lesson is to become self-emptied and God-filled. Humanity progresses in this school through many grades encompassing lifetimes. There are innumerable examinations to be passed and degrees of advancement to be earned. The supreme wayshower is The Lord Emmanuel. His archetypal life impressed its pattern upon the future of man's spiritual evolution and since then a steady stream of His emissaries have been scattered thinly but mightily from age to age. Their light, like single torches in the darkness, has made all the difference to the hundreds and thousands who yearn to climb up out of the caves of spiritual ignorance. Because they have always been few in number their value as wayshowers has made them precious. Their radiance, when caught in the lives they change, is reflected in the history of humanity's enlightenment. For those who are baptized with this Divine fire, its touch ignites a holy quest, causing them to rise up awake and aware.

There is a compelling need to share glimpses of this flame with the distant world and books are written that history will not forget a St. Francis of Assisi or a St. Teresa of Lisieux in whatever age they appear. But the outlook of history is the past and it is easily forgotten that now is one of humankind's most momentous ages. This, then, is the story of two such persons in present time and what happened and still happens.

Chapter 1

Early Lifetimes in Peru and Egypt

On the dimly lit horizon of civilization in the Andes mountains of South America, some thousands of years ago, flourished a Pre-Incan people about whom humanity has lost all trace. They were forerunners, a creative band of Indians living ahead of their times and breaking ground for the great cultural advances in the millennia to follow. It was a simple life with the accent on mystic ritual and moral conduct; the visibly spectacular achievements of government, architecture and military conquests would wait until much later, distinguishing the Incas. The work of these earliest settlers was to lay the spiritual foundations of all cultures to come after them, and this was done.

Their life resembled the nomadic Indians who roamed the plains of North America centuries later though they had none of the warlike fierceness of the plains tribes. Their features also were strikingly more Asiatic, having ventured so recently from that continent. What they left behind is known in two ways: reflections among their descendants of a reverence for nature—preeminently, worship of the sun—and impressions surviving in the memory of one who was there.

Fourteen lives ago, in view of awesome Mt. Chimborazo where the country of Ecuador now lies, a woman named Flower began her pilgrimage on earth. There were no cities or man-made enterprises to divert her people from a simple quest: spiritual enlightenment. Her first clear memory is of a migration to the area of Lake Titicaca in what is today Peru. Here, in the vastness cradling the waters of this holy place,

13

was nurtured one of the earliest mystery schools on earth. Lingering with her still is the vivid imagery of a small group of men and women gathered in council and conducting rites about a glorious chief. She was one among a few maidens who were chosen to share in these esoteric teachings and who held responsibilities similar to vestal virgins. The chief was a soul far advanced and deeply wise. The particular details of the doctrines he taught have since faded from her memory, but she will never forget his spiritual nobility.

He had a daughter, a princess, who was her closest companion and a great help to her in an unusual way. Until this first human incarnation, Flower had evolved through the Angelic line of evolution. As she would later teach in the twentieth century, upon reaching a certain point of advanced rank, this Kingdom allows its citizens the choice of continuing toward Godhood as an Angel—a path which is unobstructed but gradual—or to cross over to the human line of evolution where growth is arduous but greatly accelerated. She chose the latter and was overwhelmed by the multitude of strange adjustments earth life imposed. The princess seemed to understand her need for coaching and was an invaluable friend.

Along with the challenges, there were bright moments when her Angelhood shone through to delight those around her. It was the custom among the maidens to gather in small groups of never more than four, sharing impressions of the inner side of life. Coming from such a light-filled world, her unique perceptions of things around her intrigued the others. Flower's luminous sensitivity touched dimensions unknown to her companions: revelations of Angelic presences, hidden wonders in nature, the discovery of beauty in everything, and, most of all, a capacity for spiritual love that knew no bounds.

But the unfamiliar vessel of a body was a great undertaking, along with the alien elements of human nature and ways of thinking. The princess was tireless in helping Flower with

14

these difficulties, each time sensing her singular needs.

The days passed drenched in sunlight from above and within. They were busy always; duties were carefully assigned by the chief, blending inner work with the practical tasks of living in an otherwise primitive world. One feeling permeated all that they did, however. It was the sense of preparation underlying each devotional duty and every earthly task. There was no idle activity or any feeling of drifting comfortably through pleasant self-contained days. They were making themselves ready; for what they were unsure except to know its immanent importance.

Then a day came when the chief called them together and asked that they collect their bare essentials for the beginning of a pilgrimage. They set out on a trek that was to last many years. Its purpose was for spiritual initiation; it took them to distant places known or revealed to their wayshower for inner reasons. The journey became so lengthy, she no longer remembers how it ended or whether she ever returned from its ordeals. The distance covered in such high altitudes took enormous stamina and the hazards they faced from hostile tribes, the precipitous terrain, wild animals, and privation, clung like shadows to their footsteps. There is a final, fleeting impression of going out of this life struggling in an effort to follow the princess she loved and admired. Whether it was an initiatory rite or one of the frequent emergencies encountered in their travels is forgotten; all that remains is the intense sensation of that last grasp of life.

The most valued gain of this incarnation was the transcendent instruction of the magnificent priest-chief making it possible for her to bridge the world of Angel with that of man. It was to give her the footing needed for a still longer journey across lifetimes when she would bring forth a teaching in her own right on the western shores of the sister continent to the north. That would be the time of the New Age with its teachings made more marvelous by the wealth of things to come.

☙ ✳ ❧

After Peru, Flower passed through a succession of eight lifetimes encompassing many centers of civilization, but those leaving the strongest impressions were India, China, Chaldea and Yucatan. Some of these embodiments were needed to gain better grounding in the earth environment and its cultural forms: others were spent in the direct pursuit of mystical channelship and mystery teachings. But throughout all of these lives a single theme reoccurred: character—always, endlessly, character. It required the discipline of spiritual integrity in keeping one's consciousness increasingly centered on God and the discipline of self-givingness in one's relationships with others and service to Divinity. So essential, so overwhelmingly first was this prerequisite to discipleship that its archetypal qualities formed the gates of every major and minor initiation through to Mastership.

She began the final stages of preparation for her own life work when in Egypt near the conclusion of the eighteenth dynasty. A 16-year old pharaoh had just been crowned, changing his name from Amenhotep IV to Ikhnaton. The year was 1369 B.C., and marked an auspicious occasion not only for Egypt, but for all of humankind. This pharaoh, the greatest of the Egyptian rulers, was about to announce the revelation of one God, absolute, supreme, and the solitary Creator of heaven and earth. In the same year he took as his wife the beautiful Nefertiti, his constant companion since childhood, and together they would write a unique chapter in Egyptian history. In one of the most sweeping cultural revolutions of all time, not just religion but every aspect of civilized life was rekindled overnight along a sheltered bank of the Nile untouched by previous dynasties. The empire of Ikhnaton burned like a

16

consuming flame for sixteen years, after which Egypt would violently extinguish the light of this splendid renaissance and return to the shadowy underworld of its own changeless past.

The bold pronouncements of the young pharaoh caught the established priesthood in shocked surprise. Their reaction was first disbelief, then bitter resentment. Who was this royal upstart to usurp their powers, undermine their privileged positions, and relegate their gods to oblivion?! Such a man either must be mad or out to seize everything for himself, beginning with the gods. It hardly mattered which—in blind rebellion to keep hold of the Egyptian mind through the binding complexities of a pseudo-religious tyranny based on death, magic, and bribery, they began a long and deadly struggle.

The outcome would seal the fate of Egypt's future like a great vented tomb where life would linger in the flickering lamplight of an unchanging illusion of reality. Yet before this man-made twilight fell over the length of the Nile world, Ikhnaton illuminated a moment of history beyond belief. So incredibly original was his genius—and so complete the campaign to eradicate its mark—that modern archeologists would be dumbfounded to uncover its secret wonders silently waiting in the rubble of a forgotten place named Amarna. When Ikhnaton foresaw that Thebes was unalterably resistant to the revelations of his reign, he made a decision: he would build an entirely new capital, with its own architecture, art, manner of living, and, most revolutionary of all, a new religion worshiping the one God, Aton. Contrary to everything in the tradition of the gods, Aton demanded no sacrifices, made no menacing threats, and fostered no fearful superstitions. Of the forty-two laws in the traditional code of Egyptian ethics which provided the net for a corrupt priesthood to entangle the populace, the one God answered simply, "Love transcends law!"

In art, as in religion, Ikhnaton wanted this new city to help men set aside their illusions and see things as they really

17

were. Art suddenly spoke with a refreshing realism and a simple beauty. Sculpture and mural painting no longer distorted the size or features of subjects or the appearance of scenes to fit the exaggerated preconceptions of the ruling class, and buildings, especially the temples, expressed a lovely simplicity of line and quiet nobility that inspired, rather than intimidated, the onlooker.

In a score of months the wondrous city of Amarna arose from the virgin wilderness at a point along the Nile halfway between Thebes to the south and Memphis to the north. The setting was an imposing valley sheltered by great natural walls of rock, a site thoughtfully chosen by Ikhnaton to create the earth's first master-planned city. Everything from the tastefully decorated homes of workers to the charming palace rooms of the royal family sprang forth under his brilliant direction

Amarna was known as a city of gardens and flowers. Every home was decorated with hanging baskets of exquisite blossoms and each woman in the royal household had her own private garden in which to rest and worship. The principal household belonged to Nefertiti, Queen of Egypt, and Ikhnaton's favorite, but there were other wives in the royal family to strengthen the pharaoh's line and increase the circle of his court. One of these, his fourth wife, gave him a daughter who was Flower. In a few years, while still a young girl, she would enter the temple for training and begin her instruction in the mystery school of her extraordinary father.

Her early childhood passed in the warm happiness of the royal family basking in the sunlight of a golden age in the fragrant gardens of a miraculous city. Childhood was mostly a time of waiting until the doorways of her maturity opened wide enough to step out onto the path of attainment once again. Though much had been transformed, the reign of Ikhnaton was no utopian dream, free of human frailties—not

18

even for his own court or household. Her first memories were of a large palace and its intricate court proceedings, a phenomenon that greatly fascinated her. In spite of the pharaoh's success in refashioning so many of the complexities and false appearances of Egyptian life, the subtle craving of his subjects for pomp and intrigue persisted in subdued measures; even among his wives evolved an envious game, each maneuvering for a position of advantage over the other. But the deadliest of contests went on, of all places, in the temples of the new religion.

One daughter from pharaoh's line was chosen to represent him in a life of dedication in the temples. When Flower was just entering her teens, she was elected by her father to serve in this way and begin the intensive training he wished. The first lesson was unexpected and chilling: between the teachings of Ikhnaton and the practices of the priests lay a frightening gulf. While some were genuine converts to monotheism, accepting the new values eagerly, many others were engaged in a conspiracy to undermine the Pharaoh and rescue all the vices they had grown to prefer. Pretending loyalty to his office and exploiting every opportunity of their position otherwise, they engaged in an insidious duplicity, grasping or groveling for power and privilege as in the old days. It was this corrupt element that had finally penetrated even the sanctuaries of Aton. Only Flower's standing as a daughter of royalty protected her from the sexual abuses forced upon temple maidens routinely. There were, among the priests, a few of sufficient courage and skill to give inestimable help during periods of danger. One in particular did everything possible to safeguard her in perilous situations. He was the assistant to the most villainous of all—the head priest, diabolically perverse, and one of the few men Flower ever remembers despising.

Against this background of darkness were multitudes

of shining moments making up the harvest of this incarnation, all gathered from the teachings of Ikhnaton. These she plunged into with her heart's whole enterprise, for they necessitated intense work. He taught her how to enter a state of semi-consciousness during which she could leave her body and observe reality from the inner side, describing the events she beheld. Music accompanied this experience, trumpets and lyres predominantly, and dense vapors of incense filled the room. She learned in this way to foretell coming events which were of great interest to Ikhnaton.

Another significant dimension of her training was in the dance, an activity forming a prominent part of the new religion's worship. This was a joyous duty, and being one of the temple dancers brought through a deepening awareness of how rhythm and movement, when performed reverently, draw both performer and beholder closer to God.

When her father finally died her life was in immediate jeopardy and the outcome of this crisis lies beyond her recollection. Whatever happened, none of it subtracted from these resplendent experiences of learning that were forever hers. She would see this most unforgettable of men again in the most unbelievable of attainments. He ruled Egypt as its most enlightened pharaoh and had another incarnation as David, King of Israel. She would meet him next in Palestine when he became the first to attain the highest pinnacle of human evolution—Christhood. Before that transcendent realization, Flower would have two more lives.

Chapter 2

Journeying Through Persia and Greece

There are rhythms to the spiraling wheel of evolution which blend distinctive themes into a balanced whole and space periods of assimilation between the upward slopes of rapid growth. Flower knew such a life in Persia during the incarnation of Zoroaster. At first, her circumstances were rather ordinary; she was a young housewife with two children before anything of memorable importance took place. Then, quite suddenly, her husband died, and the heartbreak of this loss drew her into the orbit of Zoroaster's teachings. How pure they were! It was like being awakened from a restful sleep by a clear, shining ray of sunlight breaking through morning mists. Her sadness gradually slipped away as she drank in the renewing words of this great one's immaculate wisdom.

Zoroaster taught the spiritual necessity of purification and much of his training aimed at ways to purge his pupils from the hold of their lower natures. With purification came the quickening awareness of Divinity in all things, and this was his gift to all who came to learn. It was in nature that Zoroaster found the living model of purity. His love for this world of creatures and growing things, ever in the process of cleansing and rebirth, was delightfully infectious. His profound kinship with the nature realm brought her to an appreciation of animals and walks in nature exceeding anything previously felt. She had always been closely attuned to these spheres but he provided the insight linking reverence for nature directly to a man's ascent toward God. To become a part of this world of primal creation is to know one's own loving obligation to the Life Principle in everything. That was his momentous secret and her bright heritage.

ᘗ ✳ ᘘ

The sixth century before Christ was struck by a bolt of celestial fire setting off an avalanche of unparalleled light. In a span of 32 years, five of the earth's most celebrated teachers breathed the air of the same supercharged atmosphere though, except for the two from China, they never met and were separated by thousands of miles. Beginning with Zoroaster in Persia, the sunburst of enlightenment spread to Lao-Tse in China, Pythagoras in Greece, then Guatama Buddha in India, touching once more the mountain tops of China with Confucius. If ever there was a time for compressing the space between incarnations it was now.

Flower had scarcely concluded her life as a Persian, rapt in the beauteous wisdom of Zoroaster, when she set out on another pilgrimage that was to be her favorite, most fulfilling incarnation. The country was Greece and her teacher, the Master Pythagoras.

She was born into a family of means, her father being prominent in the political affairs of that country. The years of childhood passed quickly and when she was seventeen she was granted her heart's desire: entrance to the finest academy of its time, the mystery school of Pythagoras located at Delphi near the foot of Mt.Parnassus. She vividly remembers her first meeting with the Master, for as he greeted her he recognized at once that, beyond her human form, she was a native of the Angelic Kingdom. His salutation opened a door that would never close again, and as these happiest of days blossomed, she realized Pythagoras was more than a teacher—he was her spiritual father helping to give birth to propensities within her that other lives had carefully conceived. How glorious it was to feel this emergence! To be alive at such a time! To be a pupil in his extraordinary school!

Pythagoras was 45 when Flower entered his Academy. Already he had traveled extensively throughout the world of his day visiting Persia, Crete, Palestine and India. He was a tall, powerfully built man with broad, graceful shoulders. His hair was a medium brown, with streaks of iron-gray, and hung loosely to his shoulders. He had large gray eyes which sometimes seemed blue and always they penetrated the very depths of the soul who fell into his gaze. His face was free of lines, even to the end of his life, there was about him a commanding dignity and presence—he was a Master through and through.

To the outsider an impelling fascination surrounded the Academy of Pythagoras. Being a mystery school, its doors only opened to the devout candidate after a vigilant screening and the personal sanction of the Master. Once inside, the student was pledged to secrecy regarding the school's training methods and esoteric curriculum, a tradition that kept the world ignorant of facts about the Academy and its founder. Even his orthodox teachings were not written down in his lifetime and the methods which brought illumination to so many of his disciples were never revealed to the world.

Pupils were of two kinds: single individuals who remained for life, and married couples forming the household group who stayed through the basic instructional cycle of ten years, then returned to the outside world to exemplify the way. Everyone spent the first five years in silence, speaking only in answer to questions from the instructors. The couples lived separately, obedient to chastity, mingling together during the services and classwork.

For Flower, the years slipped by unnoticed in her joyous embrace of these luxuriant hours. Singing instantly became her favorite activity, all pupils being trained to chant their frequent devotions in lovely, lyrical melodies. Some were sung in solemn, hushed tones, but most were vibrant with gladness, swelling with praise to the Most High. How she loved the fusion of voices rising together in waves of glorious sound; she never tired of the happy necessity to create the endless tide of music, rising and falling, day after day.

But there was more. Pythagoras beheld in music the language of the spheres and he taught his pupils to listen with the inward ear, catching the hidden signals; glimpsing the inner scenes brought to life by these silver-toned chords. Sometimes dancing, performed by the household group, would transform the strains of music into bird-like flights of human movement.

Instruction in his school began with philosophy presented at different levels. A major foundation of his teachings was reincarnation, but a far more enlightened view of the ring of rebirth than history records. He never taught the false doctrine of transmigration often attributed to him: the notion that man returns to earth in animal forms. His teachings, so wrongly confused with the older Orphic traditions, were fresh revelations of truth that formed much of the basis of modern esoteric knowledge and were encyclopedic in their scope.

When Pythagoras lectured, it was usually in a circular area, out-of-doors. At its center was a rectangular sand pit in which he drew the illustrations of his lesson. He was insistent on the quality of presence of mind: the alert, perceptive keenness of thought that both analyzed and synthesized information swiftly and clearly. The tool he developed for this purpose was intuition, the immediate awareness of truth through the direct sensing of the interior essences of things.

Of all subjects, mathematics was the mainstream of Pythagoras' genius and its study was given a prominent place in the school's curriculum. There were long exercises in this discipline, followed by searching inquiries into the nature of numbers and their relationship to the design of the universe. Flower remembers struggling with these complexities while the Master smiled in unconcealed amusement: his sense of humor was a welcome relief at such a moment of trial.

Pythagoras was a perfectionist whose standards always seemed beyond the reach of others, yet his high expectations became the driving force propelling the pupil past ordinary limits into the thin, sweet air of unrealized conquests. He was painstakingly precise about the manner of one's speaking. He measured each word for its fitness in a sentence, calling a pupil's attention to weak or inaccurate usage and suggesting a more suitable phrase. The tone and quality of one's voice were meticulously noted, then matched with a coaching regime to draw out the most correct and pleasing speech.

The working day was 10 full hours, moving between classes and activities in a rhythmic flow of absorbing occupation. There was an ease to the program that never became casual; an orderliness that was never mechanical. As busy as the days were, she felt the sweet, warm happiness of being deeply, consecratedly, joyously in love with life, and the great fortune of studying at this most enlightened of learning centers. Pythagoras had gathered about him a dedicated, gifted faculty. Two, a man and a woman, stand out in Flower's memory, so close were they to the threshold of Mastership. The woman possessed a rare classical beauty and was an exceptional teacher. The man was her equal as a teacher; together, they had the magic that turned ordinary hours into moments of living time: he has since become the Hindu Master Shallwanawaki. There was also Theoclea, the wife of Pythagoras—the most incredibly beautiful woman she had ever seen.

These first ten years seemed gone in half the time, laying into place an educational foundation of vast dimensions. The numerous couples of the household group reluctantly departed now, but for Flower it was the beginning of unimagined openings into the inner worlds. With the cornerstone secured the architect signaled the commencement of the temple of her extended clairvoyance with its windowed walls and skylighted ceiling looking out from above the vapors of the earth upon the mystic hills and heavens of the inner worlds.

The work centered upon a wholly new form of deep meditation, allowing her to step out of her body with surprising facility and to remember everything clearly on her return. All the preparation in other incarnations now converged to a single stream of illumined consciousness: she was awake as never before, aware upon the command of her will. How glorious it was!

Pythagoras rejoiced in her skill and personally directed the training. The moment was memorable, and the dream of every teacher: to find the pupil with an unequaled talent, who is teachable, and who will give herself unsparingly to the goal. He intensified the instruction to fit his exacting standards, rooting out mediocrity and pruning every flaw. He had patience only for excellence and always he pressed for more. When she had given her utmost in describing clairvoyantly some interior phenomenon, he would show great interest and probe still deeper:

"Yes," he would say, "but there must be more. Look farther; haven't you missed something? Describe it once again, carefully. I'm sure there must be more."

And there would be! His intuition was uncanny in the way it pierced through to an absent element or an incomplete detail. And still more questions: there seemed to be no way to satisfy him. Her mind served him like a camera lens, penetrating the mysteries of the other side of life.

His own clairvoyance was unlike hers, making Flower's unique sensitivity to these inner realities all the more fascinating to him. Noteworthy of Pythagoras was his ability to perceive intuitively just what were another's thoughts and recognitions in a given attention field. He knew immediately, under his relentless probing, when at last she glimpsed the correct perspective and gained the sharpest focus.

The time soon came when he found her wholly trustworthy. Then, together, they began an extensive exploration of the Akashic Records: she, the researcher gathering the data, and he, the scholar, brilliantly synthesizing the vast treasury of information. Two formidable tests had to be passed to approach the Records. The first was mastery of the highest order of clairvoyance; the second, and most crucial—absolute spiritual *integrity*. Pythagoras knew the gateways to these imperishable memory traces were guarded by two blindingly iridescent Archangels. No candidate could pass without their infallible scrutiny. All of her training in every previous incarnation, the ten years of preparation in his mystery school, the final years of accelerated tutoring under his personal charge—suddenly coalesced in the alchemy of this transcendent opening and, like crystals at a melting point, irreversibly lost all opaqueness to the clear splendors of inner fire. His gift to her was a conscious, far-seeing clairvoyance, unclouded and at her immediate command. It required no trances and never possessed her: she simply saw unimpededly with the Third Eye in a way that was singular and unique.

What drew Pythagoras' interest most in the Akashic records were the past incarnations of pupils and other significant persons as the meaning of their lives became unveiled by the law of cause and effect. His empirical spirit gave to mysticism a practical relevance, while his grasp of mathematical truth gave it precision and orderliness. Gradually, the reconstruction of the inner worlds took form in an elegant esoteric doctrine, the most far-reaching of its day; one that would become a permanent part of the world's mystical heritage.

Pythagoras was one-pointed about living by spiritual rules and with his goal of accurate authentic channelship went a rule of far-reaching significance: *immediate, total obedience to inner instruction.* Whatever came through from Divinity, it must be obeyed here and now, to the letter. For every pupil he trained, this was at once the most severe and marvelous commandment.

"Why am I training you to be channels of the Light?" he queried. And answering his own question, "So that you can be the servants of God and do His Will." The personal thrill of extrasensory experience for its own sake was never permitted. Yet, not until the contacts were open and the instructions began streaming through did the neophyte realize the burden of this power. It was like growing up all over again. Children dream of what it will be like one day to win a grownup's privileges and freedoms only to reach adulthood, looking back with a nostalgic tug on the days of carefree innocence. It was the same with clairvoyance; the marvels of the interior worlds brought not only unimagined beauty, but Divine commands and a profound grasp of responsibility. To listen and fail to obey the inward voice; to see and not to act upon the glimpse of heaven—and to act—never for the self, but solely for the good of all humanity—that was the dark failure risking everything. Having heard the music of the spheres, seen the splendors of inner creation, then touched by this magic, ever to be imprisoned from it: that would be the unspeakable agony.

These tragedies were unknown at the Academy. The first disciplines Pythagoras instilled into his pupils were those of character and duty. Not until the novitiate proved himself beyond doubt did the arduous quest of sensory illumination begin. Its course led directly to the higher planes of awareness safefolded in the armor of meditative alignment. There were no seances or other excursions into the world of spirits or astral phenomena. The single purpose was to become a conscious instrument of God's will for the advancement of humanity.

Flower always was with the Master, though they had long since left Greece. Delphi was also the site of the politically prestigious oracle and the reputation of Pythagoras aroused envy and suspicion among its priests and the power elite, who mounted a campaign of terror that ended in the seizure and burning of the Academy. Foreseeing these acts, he had warned his people, and most escaped to Crotona, Italy, where the relocated school flourished, rising to the zenith of its attainment. Within its peaceful walls Flower came to the finest accomplishments yet known to her evolution in close, adoring kinship with her Master.

Her work kept her in the midst of the training activity all of her life, never requiring that she leave the Academy. But there was a continual need to seek out new believers wherever they might be found. Here or there, in a small village or crowded city, an individual waited to hear the few words that would awaken his soul's memory and bring him to his spiritual home. It was not the masses Pythagoras sought as followers, but the handful of candidates at the brink of discipleship, ready to loosen their attachments to outward circumstances, take their vows and become his pupils.

Regularly, certain of the men would set out in small bands like troubadours, going from place to place, singing of their way of life and conversing with the onlookers they attracted. Some of the women trained in drama also toured the land, performing plays whose stories skillfully interwove twin themes. One had a light, pleasing motif to entertain the general populace; the other hid its message from the view of all except an alert brother or sister who, catching the secret meaning, hurried forward at the end to become one of the group.

All of these activities required robust health. Pythagoras undergirded his pupils with a regime of exercise and diet that assured strength and durability in carrying out their duties. Gymnastics was a regular feature of each day's routine, with the accent on the body's grace and poetry of movement. Food never became a faddish or rigid matter. Their meals consisted of a wholesome variety of dishes tastefully prepared and enjoyed against a background of lovely music from a lyre or flute.

Deeply impressed upon Flower were the values of beauty, cleanliness, order, and refinement that permeated every activity. One's personal appearance never could be neglected and great care was invested in cultivating meticulous habits. To do anything for the Master in a religious way, everyone wore their finest vestments. When they would assemble on these occasions, the sight of so many soft, flowing robes blending together in delicate pastel shades fashioned an exquisite picture.

At the evening meal, along with their fastidious attire, they unobtrusively practiced immaculate manners, gracious conversation and living the Way. Often, the Master and others within the circle of teachers would share personal reflections that brought them closer to their pupils out of the spontaneity and brotherhood of the setting. Nor was there any lack of mirth. Discipline was the basic condition for growth, the essential lawfulness making all other aspirations possible; but joyousness was its counterpart. The school was structured to insure the success of its pupils, if they were steadfastly willing to give themselves. And because they did, they grew: therein was their rejoicing! The atmosphere was earnest, never somber; cheered by warmth and good humor, without becoming frivolous. Nor was Pythagoras ever facetious, yet he sparkled with laughter over the little human idiosyncrasies that frequently projected out of the lives of his pupils, like unruly branches to trip upon. His demonstration was to laugh freely at one's self, the sooner, then, to be finished with pride and vanity.

Flower had no unpleasant memories of this life, in spite of the enormous hostility Pythagoras and his school aroused among the materialistic, power-motivated factions that drove them from Delphi and later brought destruction upon Crotona itself. In the end, these engineers of violence murdered large numbers of his followers and scattered the rest into distant exile. Those who escaped were like fagots from a hearth fire, igniting the esoteric hearthstones of the old world for a time, then banking their coals until later incarnations. This was the great legacy of Pythagoras: a host of incandescent souls lighting their way through the oncoming ages, rekindling the truths he supplied them in the mystic tinder of future generations.

The end for Pythagoras, Flower and many others was tragic, yet the details were never important. Her last sight of him was with snow-white hair; and of herself, she only remembers dying around the age of 35. So brimming with accomplishment was this incarnation, so rich the impressions of Divinity and so transcendent the openings into the inner worlds, no mark of sadness survived. What an extraordinary life it was to have intimately known two worlds and such a Master—then to step out of the earth so lightly, not to have felt death.

Chapter 3

The Wonder of Palestine

Her incarnation with Pythagoras was like a warm summer day in a lovely alpine meadow: everything green and bursting with life; her work delightful. The sunlight, in particular, was soft and lucid, enhancing everything in sight. It was unforgettable; so beautifully right and purposeful.

The sun that shone upon Palestine, in contrast, was of such a brilliance all else paled to insignificance. Places took on little importance and people stood in the background, awestruck by the unearthly radiance of a single individual: the Lord Christ.

Flower was born in Bethany, a village near the foot of Mt. Olivet east of Jerusalem. Her own mother was a lifelong companion of Mary's, the two having grown up together in this village. At Flower's birth Mary became her godmother and both families drew even closer together until the death of her mother when Flower was six years old. From this time on Mary adopted her and she was raised in the family of Jesus.

None of them knew his mission, yet they were spellbound by his presence. It misses the mark to describe him as unique or extraordinary. He was unheard of, beyond understanding, and the fact of his reality had to be recaptured by seeing him, listening to him, beholding the impossible truth of his existence, over and over. When out of sight, he seemed like a figure lingering after a vision, a wondrous visitor from another world. He confounded every generalization known to the psychology of the times. Nothing explained his mystery and everything lost validity before his truth. No one could contain him in their preconceptions and all fell silent before the supernatural power of his wisdom. Yet, other than being what he was, Jesus called no sensational attention to himself throughout his youth and was mostly unknown outside of Nazareth.

He traveled often with Joseph, his father, awaiting the time when his internal forces would be ready. He never visited the schools of Egypt, India or any other land, a claim often made by those who fail to understand who he was. As Ikhnaton, he had founded the greatest of the Egyptian mystery schools, and as David he had given the Hebrew peoples their most enlightened leadership, their richest treasury of hymns to God. India was of another path and had no bearing on his mission. There was a simple, momentous fact about Jesus, visible in his face and manifest in his works: he entered life a Master and stood at the threshold of Christship. He alone, of humanity, had come to this place. He had nothing further to learn of life, was never overshadowed by any other individuality, and needed no teacher except God. His youth was a time of waiting, nothing more, and he passed it engaged in the commonplace activities of his family and the occasional journeys of his father.

Among the people close to Flower outside Jesus' family, was Mary, the sister of Martha and Lazarus. Her ways were loving and gentle and her devotion to Jesus unexcelled. Lazarus was another; an exceptionally handsome man with a large, masculine physique. He never married, performing as a professional entertainer all of his years.

Life for Flower began its quest when she was eighteen and still living with Jesus' family in Nazareth. He was thirty and had recently set out about his Father's business, calling together his disciples. Her favorite was James, the older son of Joseph, now known as the Master Amiel. He had just returned from being with Jesus and learning what people were saying about him. He poured out the news solemnly, with a sense of what it foreshadowed.

"This is what we always knew would happen," he said, describing the dramatic pronouncements made by his half-brother and the events that quickened about him. Then an ominous look came over his face and his voice fell to a cautious whisper: "But Jesus is playing with fire—he will be killed for what he plans to do."

In that electric moment, they all awakened to his mission. Gone was the puzzlement, the speculation, the wonderment about his destiny. James' words struck through like a razor of lightning. This was the Messiah promised of old! The tranquil routine of life vaporized. Deep within each of them stirred a second pulse beating to the rhythm of a new life, no longer their own. That night there was no sleep for anyone. Each lay awake vibrant with thought, somehow trying to fit themselves into an unfamiliar world so swiftly created by the news James had shared. What would become of Jesus? Of them? At first, he simply had seemed miraculously gifted—too luminous to be like anyone else yet too visible to be unreal. Now he had changed their world into a breathtaking, revolutionary creation and the past no longer existed for them. All that remained was a sense of immanence: the feeling that came to those who first saw the evening skies lighted by the Star of Bethlehem. Intuitively, the earth never again could be the same, but just how it would be different, that must await unknown events.

When at last he returned home briefly the change was apparent. It was not in his face, which had always been light-filled; nor in his stature, still as commanding as ever. It was in his movements and direction. The tempo was now more deliberate, his actions clearly aimed at a goal he alone beheld. Before, there had been a patience about him as of one waiting peacefully. Now his manner was one-pointed, intentional.

35

Days that had once passed at a leisurely pace now found their hours measured: events multiplied at a phenomenal rate. And the people came; a steady stream of visitors seeking his whereabouts, asking of his mission, begging favors to gain his audience.

There was another difference Flower noticed: his relationship to Mary. He seldom spoke to her anymore, expressing his great love with the frequent smiles she cherished. He seemed to sense her longing to cling to him more than she should. Knowing the future and the indivisible nature of his task, this was his way of helping her meet what must be.

In spite of what was upon him, Jesus never carried a burden. Art work that portrays a suffering, heavy-laden figure dishonors the reality of his matchless bearing. His lips most often were upturned and his eyes filled with merriment and a delightful, outshining humor; they revealed to all the joy of one who knows the incomparable beauty of the inner worlds. As David, they were a violet hue, but now his eyes were brown with occasional glints of violet when the light caught them just so. His hair was auburn, its wavy, reddish-brown folds shimmering in the sun. It came down well over his forehead with the sides trimmed two or three inches from his shoulders. His skin was fair, untanned for the most part, but free of pallor. He was tall without being heavy, reaching a height of at least six feet two inches.

To see him approaching sent a flash of wonder throughout one's being. No man had ever walked the earth with his power to immediately command a situation with a kindly look, a soft word or simply his presence. When he spoke of what he knew, it sent spinning sensations down the spines of his listeners, as if their very atoms were reconfigured by the impact of his truth. To look into his eyes! There was no preparation for that encounter—to see his soul face to face. No façade, no ego, none of the ordinary appearances that tell one human that another much like himself is inside. It was like gazing into an open furnace of fiery gold against which no footing could save the beholder from being consumed. Yet to be melted down by the flames of his love was a fortune beyond price.

The three years of his ministry were the most compressed and fateful in the earth's history; never again would the future course of humanity be rewritten with such authority and permanence. When the agony of the end fell, it came like the disappearance of the sun in the heavens. Life without him was sunless, spiritless, without hope. Now the miracle of his existence and the world he created through the Cause he served, were both gone. It was unthinkable not to find him again; impossible to go back to a life without him.

Then he returned as he said he would! The shock and bewilderment of the crucifixion vanished and, as the Lord Christ, he spoke to them. Until his death, only the Twelve had received his inner teachings but now he instructed them to gather as a band of Seventy, forming his mystery school for the first time. The number included about thirty women; among them, Flower. He would come and appear before the group and all could see him. He stressed reincarnation and its validity, along with the initiations. His term for the latter teaching was not the same; instead, he used the analogy of going from "gate to gate," stressing the necessity of passing through many gates to qualify for the Work. Between the gates lay the great spaces of unfinished tasks.

In these returns, he would open up the inner worlds, saying, "If you can see me, you can see others." On one of these occasions they saw a large group of Adepts and other citizens of the eternal worlds observing them. They were greatly impressed.

Among the mystery teachings that flooded out upon them, The Lord Christ emphasized the Angel Kingdom and the monumental work these selfless beings fulfilled. His statement, "I have other sheep which are not of this fold," was in recognition of their reality. He foresaw representatives prepared to teach humanity about them, and one indeed was ready, receiving from him her ordination to serve this cause in a life that would wait nearly two thousand years.

The training was swift and concentrated. Every fiber of attention strained forward that nothing be missed. The Seventy all had known lives of intensive preparation, a background that made it possible to grasp his meaning with intuitive directness. Each appearance was followed with a discussion of his newest revelations, arranging them into the order of all previous instruction, then carefully committing these to memory.

This most hallowed of all mystery schools soon became its own paradox, sheltering these teachings from the world. For the three unprecedented years of His ministry, the Lord Christ had directed His work predominantly to the masses. Unlike any previous wayshower, he walked among men and taught them in the fields and villages where they labored and lived. He spoke vividly and plainly, drawing analogies between the familiar experiences of their lives and the Kingdom of Heaven. His parables awakened for simple fishermen, humble shepherds and ordinary housewives the vision of another life within their reach. Above all else, this was his principal ministry: to save humanity from darkness by leading the common, unaffected people of the world out into the light. Only after this work was fulfilled, following his resurrection, did he turn to his second ministry, the Seventy. The peoples of ages to come would need these wayshowers to replenish the harvest fields of Christianity and prepare the way for the second coming. He meant by this not his physical rebirth but the dawning of the Christ Spirit in the hearts of humanity: the Christ consciousness active in all humankind. The Seventy were the *seed corn* for the first millennium; their importance, and the advanced preparation they required, was obvious.

As with all things secret, there eventually arose dissent among the uninitiated and the mystery teachings of Christ gradually were perverted or silenced. Origen, with great acclaim, taught the Christian truth of reincarnation at Alexandria and Caesarea in the third century A.D., then fell as one of its martyrs. Finally, in the year 325 A.D., the infamous Council of Nicaea extinguished the few remaining doctrines given to the Seventy.

But the seeds they gathered were infinitely more viable than reckoned by the politics of the early church. Would not the Seventy return and multiply their fruits, prospering the very body that feared them most and doing so through the avenue of rebirth—the one doctrine held most in anathema by these ignorant, arrogant patriarchs?

After the Ascension, only a few were able to see Him— Flower was one of these—but the doubts that assailed them at the crucifixion were gone. They now went forth to broadcast the Word in the Lord's name. Wherever they went the crowds received them with wonderment, begging to hear every detail of the Christ's return to earth and what it meant in their lives. Each of the Seventy spoke aflame with the Holy Spirit, engulfing their listeners in the fires of their enthusiasm. And the work spread; the following multiplied.

The success of these missions inevitably aroused Christ's enemies to action. They struck cruelly in the only way they understood against an unseen peril: blind violence. Flower was overtaken on the outskirts of a village, encircled by a taunting mob incited for this purpose, and stoned to death. Darkness has never surrendered the battlefield easily. Without sacrifice, there is no victory over the unregenerate self and martyrdom is often the sole way to expose evil's insanity and inspire the deathless quest. To prize God above life itself is the purest act of love: the moment when one lives forever.

❦ ✳ ❧

Palestine finished the lives of preparation for Flower, bringing her to the threshold of her own ministry. From the distant horizon of the Andes, across the millennia that brought her finally to the Holy Land, every step of her journey looked ahead to this goal. Two encompassing attributes distinguished the outcome: character and illumination. Set within each of these imperial crowns were a myriad of outshining jewels that would give radiance to the days of another century. She was, in a word, a mystic such as the earth had never seen; a bright messenger from another world, yet authentically Christian: steadfast in *Living the Way*, giving of herself, and utterly dedicated to His cause.

Greece was her favorite life and Palestine, the most momentous. The imprints of both incarnations were imperishably upon her now, like an aura of double rainbows.

With such a preparation, what a life work hers would be!

Chapter 4

Twentieth Century Life Begins

When a soul has spent lifetimes preparing to incarnate for the single purpose of establishing a spiritual work, what happens in the inner worlds? How do the Higher Ones come to decisions about this one's destiny and take steps to overshadow their growing up?

When the pupil's rank in character and precision in channelship is ready for this exacting commission, and the details of reentering life on earth must be formulated, that one is brought to a region of the inner worlds ruled by the Kindel Order of Archangels. It is their work to construct a plan containing the purposes, circumstances and karmic assets or obligations making up the framework of every earth-bound pilgrim's rebirth. For older souls, awake to the quest for Divinity, this occurs in close communication with the individual's Guardian Angel and those among the Hierarchy, the Masters and Lords of Life, responsible for the pupil's advancement.

As the time for this conference arrived for Flower, many far-reaching decisions loomed into view: What would be the nature of her mission? How would she serve the Cause? To what country and people would she be sent? What further preparation would she require in childhood and youth before setting out on her chosen path of service? And the family who would rear her, what should be its characteristics and circumstances to assure a suitable beginning, regain her past qualities and unfold the new dimensions of her calling?

The magnificent Kindel Angel now carefully reexamined each of her previous incarnations, marking down the significant milestones and summing up the ledger of karmic accountabilities. As the work progressed the Archangel formed a configuration of archetypal symbols, iridescent and shining, composing her life disc. It would contain the numerous keys mirroring the decisions she was now making and afterwards governing the course of her coming journey.

The Kindel Angel then presented her with a choice between three lines of service, all matching her preparation and offering equivalent outlets of spiritual expression: she could become a dancer, a singer, or a teacher of the Word. For each, a distinct set of conditions was required to reach fruition, leading off in three different directions.

All three opportunities were favorite callings of Flower's, rooted in the excellence of her past; it was not an easy choice to make. Then, hesitating no longer, she selected the way of the teacher: of the three, its path was most direct and that appealed to her. Once making this decision, the circumstances favorable to an overshadowed start fell into place.

The Archangel reminded her of the fact that in most of her recent lives she had been sheltered from the influences of the world and trained under the direct supervision of outer teachers. Neither of these situations would be possible in the approaching pilgrimage: she was expected to forge ahead on her own, dealing with the world directly. The Angel then suggested for a childhood a simple life with average parents who would not make demands that she live up to irrelevant family expectations.

Her education, for another thing, needn't be elaborate. The incarnation in the temples of Egypt and, more recently, the intensive training in the School of Pythagoras and the Band of Seventy in Palestine were equivalent many times over to a university education in the twentieth century. In contrast, her needs were practical ones: how to be self-reliant, to manage for herself, to solve the commonplace problems of life in her uncommon way.

There was also an element of uncertainty facing her. The Higher Ones would not know if she had derived sufficient inner strength to go ahead on her own toward the founding of a work in Christ's Name. Her channelship was not in question: what had to be proved were dimensions of her character involving the resoluteness to overcome obstacles, the wisdom to foresee problems and solve them effectively, the skill to become a leader of men and women, avoiding the erosive elements of ambitious rivals or divergent factions, and the courage to stand unyielding before the onslaughts of Darkness that inevitably assail the Light wherever it shines.

These were questions with outcomes, for the present, unknown. Their answers would be lived out in the years ahead.

❧ ✳ ☙

The afternoon was sunny and clean-swept by soft winds from the sea. Two six-year-old girls happily pressed against the rail of the Staten Island ferry as it made its way through the New York harbor. Suddenly, the face of one lighted up: dancing across the water were dozens of tiny water sprites. In delight, she tugged at the arm of her friend, exclaiming, "Oh, look at the beautiful fairies!"

Her companion, blind to such wonders, mistook this for a game of make-believe, gleefully responding with one fanciful invention after another. A look of puzzlement came over the first child's face. The water sprites still skimmed lightly over the waves but the things her friend described were nowhere to be seen. Then she looked into the other's eyes and was struck by a perplexing discovery—they were glancing about aimlessly—her friend was making up everything! And what really was there, bright and clear, frolicking about the sparkling whitecaps, had passed unseen for the other girl.

The first child, never before conscious of her natural clair-voyance, stood bewildered. As long as she could remember she had seen nature beings and other marvels more glorious still. She would cry out happily calling her family's attention to one spectacle or another, just as on this occasion, though as she thought of it now they never seemed to share her own exultation.

What was the difference? And this numb sensation well-ing up within her, what did it mean? Hesitantly, the truth crept toward the surface of her mind. She could feel the pressure of its startling secret against her forehead, breaking through the soft shell of her child's innocence: she saw a world that other people didn't. How could this be?

All the way home she struggled to grasp the fact of it, fi-nally taking it to bed where she lay awake long into the night. Not once did she doubt the revelations of her eyes; what caught her unaware was the aloneness of this gift: no one else to see with her. What was she to do? Reluctantly she reached a decision, painful in its wisdom: she would no longer speak of inner realities to those around her. As silently as lovely flow-ers in a secret garden, she would quietly close the gate, letting this be her own private sanctuary of blossoming splendors. It was a gate that remained closed to visitors until she was thirteen.

Six years earlier, on May 10, 1909, to an ordinary Chris-tian family in Allentown, Pennsylvania, was born this lumi-nous child. Her name was Mildred Arlene Sechler, though soon some question arose about that. Even before her sixth birthday, when still uninhibitedly sharing her inner experi-ences, she would correct her parents when speaking to her, saying: "But my name isn't Mildred, it's Flower."

Amusing as this was to her mother and father, it went no farther and for the time little Mildred stopped insisting. The uncommon nature of their daughter was visible in other incidents, too. One in particular was charmingly prophetic. It happened on a summer's day when she was only three years old. Near their home, by a curious coincidence, ran the Jordan River, a favorite playground for Mildred and her friends. A policeman on horseback, making his rounds of the neighborhood that afternoon, was alarmed to see her wading out into the water with several other youngsters where she began baptizing them. Noticing no

Mildred Arlene Sechler, born May 10, 1909

children in the group old enough to watch out for their safety, he called over, asking them to return to the river bank, but the children crowded around Mildred, ignoring him completely. Miffed by their unconcern, the tone of his voice changed to a sharp command—still they refused to budge. Finally, there was nothing left to do but ride out into the water, lift Mildred up behind his saddle and ride back to town with all of her following loyally parading after them.

A second episode about the same time also foreshadowed the future of this inimitable child. Her father raised prize-winning chickens: Rhode Island Reds and Leghorns with thirty-four loving cups proudly displayed in their living room. Mildred knew nothing of their pedigrees; to her they were something far more real: a host of adorable friends. One afternoon, when she found them unusually restless in their pens, she had a wonderful idea—why not take them for a walk? Calling her lovable St. Bernard, she opened the pens and summoned the entire flock of surprised hens and baby chicks after her. What a sight they made strolling down the alley, her dog leading the way and all the chickens clucking and chirping behind them. Not far ahead, sweeping her back porch, was one of Mildred's aunts. As the happy band approached, the startled woman called out: "Young lady, just where do you think you're going with those chickens?!"

She answered quite matter-of-factly, "I'm taking them for a walk."

That night, when her father arrived home to learn of this, Mildred suffered one of the few spankings of her life. How deserved the punishment must have seemed to her father in payment for such mischievous behavior, yet she never grasped the purpose of it, her only motive having been to please her little friends. This bond with animals even proved stronger than death. The devoted St. Bernard, after entering the heaven worlds, appeared at crisis points throughout her life, once thrusting her aside from a tarantula and, at other times, standing by her in the face of unforeseen dangers.

Childhood moved along quietly until her sixth year when her father died, leaving the mother with a modest inheritance to provide for Mildred and her older sister Beatrice. In one of these strange arrangements of destiny, Beatrice had lost her vision following an acute attack of measles when still very young. The two sisters, one blind and the other twice-seeing, now drew even closer together, helping their mother make the best of their new circumstances.

When Mildred was ten, events gained momentum. Her mother unwisely married a man who proved both extravagant and cruel. Within two years he ran through all of their money, enough to have seen the children fully grown and educated. Yet the most disheartening side of his nature was a vicious, uncontrollable temper that fed upon his frustration. What he couldn't be himself, he attacked mercilessly. All three were his targets but Mildred was the most vulnerable, often suffering savage beatings and kickings. No one else in this life would test her capacity for love as did this impulsive, neurotic stepfather.

His disastrous mismanagement of their finances coupled with his relentless search for quick riches strangely became one of the good fortunes of her life. His luck having run out in Allentown, he moved the family to Williamsport for a year and then on to Scranton where they would spend the next four years. It turned out to be the end of a dim, narrow passageway and the beginning, amazingly, of a stairway leading to the upper stories of an unsuspected mansion.

Most of her mother's family lived in Allentown: good Christians with Quaker leanings and a solid Pennsylvania Dutch background. But the family ties were too confining for one who needed to draw chiefly from interior resources, making her own way into an expectant future.

Her maternal grandmother and two aunts were the cords of this bondage. In their eyes, leaving one's family was a sacrilege. The oppressive devotion to clan, their domination over the comings and goings of even the least of their fold, meant a stifling atmosphere that threatened to ground the flights into the inner worlds awaiting Mildred. If life had simply gone on in Allentown—had her father not died—how differently she might have turned out: a musician, a writer, or with her clear, melodious voice, a singer perhaps; or even a minister in some established religious movement. None of these deflections occurred.

In every other incarnation, she had studied under the close supervision of an outer teacher: someone in human form. This time the plan was reversed. She must rediscover all of her past training through the memory-side of clairvoy-

47

ance, regain access to the inner worlds, the Akashic Records, and the Teachers of Life through her superphysical sensitivity, then blaze through the wilderness of this century a fresh, impelling pathway to God.

The conditions surrounding her upbringing sloped unmistakably toward this outcome. She was never exposed to any existing esoteric instruction; she never met a significant spiritual teacher in the outside world. She grew up in an environment free of alien influences, allowing her potentialities alone to emerge. Her circumstances were meager, often harsh, so that she would become resourceful and strong. Surrounded with little, only the greatness within could germinate and flourish—a harvest plan both simple and sure.

Yet it was not a sterile setting. Making up for the clannishness of his family, her grandfather warmly invited Mildred into the ring of his earthly enlightenment. He was a schoolteacher whose love for books created a library lining three walls of his spacious study. Years later, remembering how she valued the privilege of browsing among its volumes, he bequethed them to her on his death. In each book he had written neatly on

the flyleaf a succinct evaluation of the contents, a gift twice the worth of the books themselves. He was also the teacher of a large Bible class in one of the local churches and an accomplished musician, touching her life with the enchanting sounds of music.

Mildred was still ten when her family left Allentown. The move to Williamsport and eventually Scran-

Mildred and family in Dorney Park, PA

ton not only freed her from the unsuitable domination of her grandmother's entrenched viewpoints, it accustomed her mother, Beatrice and herself to change. The confidence they gained in following the stepfather to new places would prove to be a prized asset in just five more years when the most important move of her life would be at stake.

In the meantime, other events were about to happen. The first sign of things to come appeared in the familiar presence of her Guardian Angel bearing the orders of a new, quickening commission: "It is now my task," she announced, "to take the responsibility of your life's instruction. Henceforth, you must follow my directions, doing exactly as you are told. Have you any questions, my beloved pupil?"

From the dawn of consciousness, Mildred had been aware of this one's overshadowing reality, often seeking her help and advice; ever aware of her constant vigilance. It was an intimate companionship linked together by lifetimes. Until this moment, the Guardian's instructional role had been passive, responding to inquiries initiated by Mildred. How suddenly this was changed, like stepping from the out-of-doors of early childhood into the disciplined structure of a classroom. It reechoed an ancient wisdom: when the pupil is ready, the teacher appears.

The lessons initiated by this shining one were in the form of assignments given to her charge. Mildred was instructed to start attending the finest cultural events in the city: plays, concerts, art exhibits and visiting lecturers. Beatrice was earning money now and helped with the expenses. By this time, both her mother and sister realized that Mildred had some most unusual qualities, none self-seeking, and going along with her unpredictable inspirations always became an adventure.

The ordinary interests and standards of her home environment were now infused with the best the community of Scranton offered. Gradually with the Guardian's directions, she was exposed to most of the refinements her simple home life lacked. Her mother neither encouraged nor interfered with these undertakings, leaving Mildred free to obey her inner promptings. Where there was an expense, she often used her own money to purchase a book on etiquette or join the Elms Park church where, between the sixth and eighth grades, she attended Sunday school and belonged to its girl scout troop.

In each of these activities Mildred's Guardian systematically evaluated progress and set the next goal. New ventures were frequent. When she was in the seventh grade and receiving 25 cents a day for lunch money, she was instructed to go to the most expensive restaurants in town, there to acquire poise, graciousness and faultless manners. She would be shown to a lovely table by the headwaiter, who looked forward to her frequent visits, then order a bowl of soup with her quarter.

On the eighteenth of April, just before her thirteenth birthday, her Guardian came to her and said that from now on she must bear her soul's name: *Flower*. She was jubilant. At last the longing to be known by her true identity was fulfilled. A flurry of resistance momentarily sprang up from her mother and sister but she was quite final about the matter and they soon gave in. Such an ethereal name—so delicate and beautiful! It was of another world, befitting her exactly. That night she wrote of the event in the little diary kept for such golden moments, calling it her "spiritual birthday."

Chapter 5

The Call to California

While she was thirteen, her Guardian put her through two tests to overcome fear. The first began in an odd way. Until now, she had never contacted anything unpleasant in the inner worlds but for several days, whenever she turned on the kitchen faucet, she heard an ominous thumping sound coming through the pipes from far away. Since no one else noticed it, she inquired of her Guardian about the source of this noise. The reply was arresting: "Someday, when you are alone in the house, it will be necessary for you to invoke the overshadowing Presence of God, turn on the water, and wait to see what lies behind these sounds."

The opportunity was not long in coming. The next day, alone in the house and not wishing to postpone the ordeal, Flower approached the forbidding faucet. She closed her eyes, murmured one last prayer for courage, then turned the tap. The weird thumping sounds began their rhythmic beat immediately, approaching with menacing intensity. Like an icy wind from the underworlds, a dreadful panic swept over her. Never had she felt so seized by fear, nor such a sinking of her heart. The horrifying thing all at once was upon her. The breath in her throat was trapped in a deadly stillness. Then, out of the hideous darkness hobbled an eighteenth century sailor, an ugly peg leg thumping noisily along the passageway. He looked about himself in confusion, saying: "Oh, thank heaven I see light."

Flower noticed he wore a seaman's cap of that era with a long, dangling tassel. Then he spoke again: "Where am I?"

She looked at him, her fear dissolving into compassion. "You're in the lower astral world," she answered.

A vision of his past flashed before her. He had been pushed overboard on the high seas by an enemy he hated violently. His hate, in turn, had cast him into this darkness.

A light shining from behind caused her to turn. It was her Guardian summarizing what she must tell him: that he would remain in darkness until he forgave his enemy. He, alone, had incurred this fate by an identical act of violence in a previous life. His redemption was solely in his own hands.

As Flower spoke these words, the man's face began to change and brighten. Then an old companion stepped out from the background, leading him peacefully away, emptied of his hate.

She marveled at the contrast between the fear that began this episode and the tenderness concluding it.

A second test came while attending a party in the home of a friend and brought her unexpectedly face to face with a master of the dark path. The affair started out gaily, everyone having fun and mixing together easily. At first the uninvited stranger moved inconspicuously from one cluster of guests to another, sipping a glass of punch and keenly sizing up the people, their temperaments and predispositions. He smiled continuously, nodding his head to whatever was said and always staring intently into the eyes of the other person. Then, imperceptibly, he began shifting from the role of observer to showman. He was wiry with a slight, nimble build and as he talked he shifted from side to side, animating a steady flow of chatter that immediately drew all attention to himself. What he said made little sense but the way he said it enthralled the gathering. He emanated a kind of mesmeric charm that stealthily captivated everyone present. Flower was astonished by his cunning as she watched the group slip under the spell of his voice and the snake-like fascination of his black, cavernous eyes.

For several minutes everyone stood motionless, stupefied by his bewitching sleight-of-hand. Then his eyes met hers. At once he recognized who she was, fixing the full force of his dark power upon her. The room seemed frozen in silence; no one breathed, caught between the collision of two wills. Flower looked directly at him, then silently commanded: "In the name of The Christ, you have no power!"

In that instant he collapsed inwardly, his face betraying defeat and vexation. The hold he possessed over the group was broken and within minutes he left the home as quietly and mysteriously as he had arrived. The hostess and her guests stood about in confusion, unwitting victims of a mass trance as incapacitating as a strong drug. How masterful had been its execution, closing in upon them like a cold, damp fog, and as they slowly came to their senses the fact of it evaporated, leaving behind a mindless interlude.

Her Guardian, in assessing these two experiences later, pointed out the necessity of facing evil like a warrior his enemy. Evil never retreats until faced with courage and victory only comes with a confrontation: to turn in flight surrenders the field of combat to Darkness.

"You must never fear evil," observed her Guardian, "and whenever it strikes, stand your ground, encompass yourself with the armor of Christ's Light; then, compromising nothing, do battle."

During these years Flower kept true to her resolve not to mention her inner experiences to others. One memorable near-exception did occur, however, soon after moving to Scranton. They were invited to attend an Irish wake observing the death of a lovely young actress, a relative of some Catholic friends in their neighborhood. The event took place in the home of the unfortunate girl's parents, her body prominently displayed in an ornate casket right in the center of the parlor. Flower had never before attended a wake and she was aghast at the laughter and endless story telling—what would the departed soul think of such an outrage?

She observed clairvoyantly the astral form of this person standing above the casket and complained to the actress' mother, pointing out how appalling the noise and confusion would be to her daughter on the other side of life. She urged her to restore order and quiet and to encourage an attitude of respect; but all of her pleas were ignored and the wake continued in full swing.

Dismayed, she looked up again at the young woman's spirit and was startled, on closer view, to see her swaying back and forth to the music, a look of pleasure upon her face. Flower left the affair quite shaken by the mysteries of life and death.

More and more, with the appearance of her Guardian, she drew nearer the time of her destiny. She was in her first year of high school now and her class assignments included a large number of written compositions. These released the floodgates of her inner reservoirs, brimming with latent rivers of knowing. Out flowed insights and experiences across the pages of her themes amazing her teachers. The depth of thought, the stirring currents of revelation, the precocious appearance of these things in one so young, moved them profoundly.

Taken by her unaccountable giftedness, three of the teachers asked if she would be willing to start a series of truth classes, meeting in their homes. It was an incident affording an impressive glimpse into the lives of preparation behind her: she, a youth having just entered her teens, sought out by her own high school instructors that they might learn of realities of which they knew nothing, but that she knew intimately. They also learned about a remarkable dividend accompanying her clairvoyance. One evening during an engrossing discussion at the conclusion of her talk, the question was raised of the "practical" value of clairvoyance. Setting aside its access to unfathomable beauty and immediate truths, she told how it was used in preparing her lessons: when reading an assignment, the passages with the most pertinent information always stood out as if underscored with a line of bright light. This saved her hours, she laughingly confessed, while her teachers looked at each other with astonishment and perhaps a trace of envy.

Her work now was underway. The years of silence about the inner worlds collapsed under the onrush of joyous outgiving. This time there were no puzzled or unfeeling reactions as once caught her off-guard years earlier when looking out from the rail of the Staten Island ferry. Her listeners sat entranced, scarcely believing possible what she had to share with them, yet edging closer in their chairs so as not to miss a word. There were things they couldn't understand but no one doubted the validity of what they heard or the authority of the one who spoke.

Childhood, with its long years of marking time, was past. Her eagerness to be about this life's mission swiftly marshaled her waiting energies and talents to action. She was awake to her purpose, her clairvoyance marvelously unfolded; she stood at full attention, awaiting only the next command.

It came in September of 1924—she was fifteen. She had been out of school a few days recovering from an illness, enjoying the warm sun and the delicious

Flower Sechler in the 1920s

freedom of youthful leisure. All of a sudden a resplendent blue light approached her in the form of a spinning sphere. At its crown was the call sign of "The Holy One," an Adept often helping her Guardian with instruction. In another three years she would learn this was the Master John, the beloved disciple, though the absence of this knowledge now subtracted nothing from the deep feeling of reverence and humility such a sight instantly evoked.

Her Guardian appeared next at one side, relaying his instruction in a simple, sweeping sentence: "I bring you word from the Master that by November eighteenth you must be in California."

California! Nothing could have been farther from her thoughts. She could scarcely wait until her mother's return from work that evening to break the news. What an incredible turn of events for the three of them! But what ever would her mother say? This instruction, as with all the rest, must be obeyed exactly. Still, one feeling ruled out any doubts about the outcome: the tone of the Master's message indicated an imminent, unquestionable fact.

That night the three sat around their supper table excitedly talking all at the same time: California! They had no family in the west, not even an acquaintance or a casual contact. But they were going. Her mother, stubborn and disappointing in so many ways, seldom went against Flower's inner guidance in a decision of this scope.

The next day arrangements were made to sell the small Magneto Sales and Service Company that represented their only remaining assets in Scranton. The mother bought three steamship tickets to Los Angeles, carefully tucking the balance of two hundred dollars into her purse for incidental expenses and the small nest egg needed to start their new life.

On November 18, after a pleasant journey by way of the Panama Canal, their ship arrived in San Pedro and the Port of Los Angeles. The first order of business was to find a place to live, then employment. With little difficulty, they rented a small cottage; jobs, however, were another matter, with few to be found. Before long their funds were exhausted.

At this moment a curious cycle of help began. A Jewish woman learned of their plight and sent word to the Red Cross for assistance. That same day, two volunteer field workers called at their home with milk coupons and a large basket of food—both were refined Jewish women. Within a week, one of them arranged a position for Flower's mother at the May Company, a Los Angeles department store owned by a Jewish family. The warmth and kindness of these two women opened up an appreciation for the Jewish culture that, while not clouded with prejudice, might never have been so vivid and personal.

Things looked more promising now, though before getting their balance financially, one more crisis arose whose solution she would treasure. Their money was entirely gone, her mother was ill and Flower needed a nickel for streetcar fare to pick up her mother's check. Having yet made no friends in the neighborhood of whom such a favor could be asked, she turned to her sister and said, "Bea, let's sit down and pray."

The two girls sat for a moment, each praying intently, when Flower felt something underneath her hand. Lifting it up she found a shiny new nickel. Her eyes widened with surprise.

"Oh," she cried out, "we can't use this nickel—its from mysterious sources."

Beatrice answered skeptically, "But if it came in that way, it could disappear in that way. Anyhow," she added, "you probably were hiding it there all the time."

Flower looked hurt and turned to her sister reprovingly, "But if that were true, I would have been on my way long ago!"

And off she went before the little miracle could be withdrawn. It marked the only time in her life anything materialized out of thin air, though there were to be many miracle-like events working through the instrumentality of people.

By the time she was sixteen, their family finances no longer could keep pace with the mounting expenses. Flower was forced to withdraw from daytime attendance at Manual Arts High School to find work, arranging to continue her education in evening classes five nights a week over the next two years. After that, to make room for new spiritual commitments, she reduced her class load to two evenings a week for another two years, eventually making up her credits.

She began work as a messenger girl at the May Company, turning over her full salary to her mother each week, receiving in return an allowance for carfare and lunches. After two years she advanced to a sales girl position in the glove department and was allowed to put half of each week's salary—five dollars—into savings. At this time, her Guardian asked her to resume the classes of instruction begun in Scranton, in Los Angeles. Working hours in the glove department were from nine to five-thirty. She would rush home, help with the evening meal and prepare either for a night course at the high school or one of the two classes she now was conducting in Truth: Wednesday evenings at Westlake Unity Center and Friday evenings in her own home.

Attending one of her lectures at the Westlake Center was a buyer for the May Company's junior department. Like so many of the benefactors of her family, she was a generous, cultivated Jewess. Hearing Flower that night was a summit experience in her life and left behind a burning question: What was such a person with a message the entire world needed to hear, doing as a salesgirl at the May Company?

By the next day she reached a solution; arrangements were made for half the amount of Flower's weekly check to be regularly removed from her own salary. Not long after this a second buyer in the same store joined in the project and, between the two, provided her with both income and independence to teach. Flower, incredibly, was free at last to devote every waking moment to her mission.

She began by lecturing five times a week: Sunday mornings and evenings at the Westlake Unity Center and three weekday classes at the Advanced Book Store and other Unity Centers in the area. Within a year, she was earning enough in her spiritual lectures to release her two benefactors from their salary contributions.

The separate kindnesses of so many Jewish women beginning soon after her family's arrival in Los Angeles deeply impressed Flower. It struck her as no coincidence that so many persons of this background were instruments for her good. Was it not God's way in helping right the balance so badly displaced in Palestine?

About now, a lovely German widow who managed the dining room of the exclusive San Markand Hotel in Santa Barbara heard Flower speak in the Westlake Center and invited her to come to that city. One other time she had been in its vicinity, spending a week in Ojai at the center founded by the eastern teacher, Krishnamurti. Coming to California on the steamer, she had met a Cuban theosophist who arranged for her expenses if she would make this brief visit and write a report to his group in Havana. She found him a man with shining integrity, surrounded by a most beautiful aura of light. His teachings, however, seemed cold and intellectual to her own training, and she never had occasion to revisit him. The outcome of this week she valued most was meeting three individuals who later became lifelong friends, helping found her life work.

But now it was the charming widow's fervent invitation bringing her back to Santa Barbara; she was keenly desirous of sharing Flower with her friends in this area and promised to make all arrangements in advance, personally guaranteeing the expenses. When the time came, a large audience had gathered filling most of the seats in Santa Barbara's principal lecture hall. Immediately the audience fell in love with her and nothing would do except she return once a month, indefinitely. A bonus went with this affectionate reception: to offset her expenses and draw closer to her, various wealthy families took turns as her host for the weekend. All of the meticulous training provided by her Guardian in Scranton now found its usefulness.

She greatly enjoyed these times, partaking of the world of elegance, listening to the conversations of people highly educated and widely traveled. But it was their thirst for spiritual enlightenment that pleased her most. Their university educations served them to a point, then abruptly ceased, demonstrating the curious fact that learning limited to the intellectual level more often camouflages truth than reveals it. Their travels and acquaintance with prominent people interested her at first, but too frequently the observations they shared were disappointing, only skimming the surface of life. About their travels, she could only imagine what wonders remained hidden from view; of the celebrities, a preoccupation with glamour and their own personalities deflected the quest for inner potentialities, causing them to search for the Shores of Divinity least of all.

What most engaged these new friends was Flower's refreshing simplicity, her unaffected, warmhearted relationship with others, the astonishing range and vividness of her clairvoyance and, when they knew her well enough, the single-mindedness of her spiritual integrity.

Some were too quick to see her as simply an angelic creature, innocent of worldly knowledge, supposing a childlike inability to cope with sophisticated matters. To their surprise, the incisive directness of her perception sliced through these complex entanglements like the sword of Alexander severing the Gordian knot. What some imagined to be the limits of her talent turned out to be her trained disinterest in such unfruitful concerns. Only those listening to her concise intonements of the essential points, letting go of their fondness for intellectual obscurities, could grasp how her enlightenment made obsolete the constructions of an earthbound consciousness.

To some, she was a novelty whose ideas were quaint but impractical, even unlikely. These disenfranchised themselves by their incapacity to break the hold of the world's thinking. To all the rest, the great majority, she was irresistibly lovable, an unobstructed channel, and a wayshower of compelling depth.

The circle of her following in Santa Barbara widened further with each visit. Her weekends still were spent in luxurious homes, mostly in nearby Montecito, and the experience of chauffeurs, butlers, and maids dimly brought back memories of her childhoods in Egypt and Greece, before entering the mystery schools of Ikhnaton and Pythagoras, when servants were plentiful.

Two of the friends she first met at Krishnamurti's Ojai center, Merle and Ruth, next made arrangements for a lecture engagement in San Francisco. The response was like Santa Barbara all over again. Their uplift to receive the outshining of her encircling love and their fascination to hear one who beheld the inner worlds was irresistible. An unlimited series of lecture visits was agreed upon and a nucleus of students quickly formed.

Gradually, she assumed responsibility for her full expenses, continuing to be the principal support of her family, giving half of whatever she earned to her mother. She was now entering the decade of her twenties. All of the earned disciplines, the extrasensory skills, and the mastery of knowledge

61

from the past were vibrantly active. The journey from her childhood in Pennsylvania to the shores of the New Age in Southern California had been accomplished, preserving her resourcefulness and initiative. She had studied under no living teachers, receiving her instructions solely from the inner side of life. All the contemporary occult doctrines, Theosophy, the Rosicrucians, and their like, were largely unknown to her. What she taught came straight from the mystery schools of her past and the ceaseless currents of Divinity active around her, comprising the food and drink of her spirit.

She had now completed her apprenticeship as a teacher and lecturer under the tireless direction of her Guardian. To the preparations of lifetimes had been added the refinements of this incarnation's childhood and youth. With all the preliminaries complete, the next ascent of God's Mountain was close at hand.

Chapter 6

Flower's Mission Received

To the ordinary observer, Flower lived in a miraculous world pulsating with superphysical life. About stones and other inanimate objects hovered filmy emanations of activity called elementals. Myriads of nature beings busily swarmed over the surface of the earth nourishing every blade of grass, flowering plant, and leafy shrub. Others of their kind tended the streams, lakes, and oceans, and still others, the airways and weather elements. The mightier presences of devas oversaw these activities for extensive nature tracts, tenderly inspiring and directing the work, forever turning the wheel of the seasons through the cycle of rest and regeneration.

Beyond these realities ranged the unspeakably wondrous inhabitants of eternity: the Angels, Archangels, Angel Princes, and hosts of other orders of beings whose names and purposes she one day would share with the world.

Through the eye of her clairvoyance she was aware of the Hierarchy: the ranks of Perfected Men and Women who, as Masters and Lords, formed the inner government of humanity. Her access to the Akashic Records drew aside the veil of the past, graphically recreating the chain of events behind every personal circumstance or cultural condition, recovering lost epochs of history, and retrieving the great unwritten truths of man's quest for wisdom.

Emanating from every person, as easily as she might note their clothing, she observed the human aura and the broadcasting of thought forms and feeling tones. This skill, especially, illuminated her work as a spiritual counselor.

Nor were her sensitivities only visual. From Angel calls to the music of the spheres streamed melodies, chords, and symphony-like passages whose beauty was impossible to imagine but once heard, left the listener immersed in an oceanic reverence. Then, from time to time, flower-like fragrances filled the inner worlds, signaling a great presence or ceremonial observance.

For three lifetimes she had known these secret realities as intimately and uninterruptedly as breathing. She had long since forgotten what once it had been like not to have known them. Yet the ingredients of the ordinary world remained about her, colorless and flat by contrast. She could recognize their effects in the impoverished glances and dulled feelings of the great masses of people.

With clairvoyance went an expansion of consciousness that permanently obliterated commonplace experience. Without taking it for granted, she saw past the surface of people and things into the heart of their superphysical essences. Possessing such a gift, remembering its qualities of radiance, enlightenment, and nearness to God, what could excel such an estate? Was she not, in fact, surrounded by heaven? Could there be anything more?

❧ ✳ ☙

For nearly a year Flower had been enjoying a new, stimulating series of adventures. A German couple who had attended her classes back in Scranton before moving west, began taking her into the mountains on weekends and holidays. It was their fondness for settings reminiscent of the German Alps that opened up to her a bright, joyous heavenworld on earth. Since coming to Los Angeles, the demands of earning a livelihood and taking up the work of a teacher more than consumed the days of a week; nor was there anyone in her family to drive a car. How much. then, she appreciated these glorious outings into nature playgrounds. Together, they visited many lovely mountain areas. But one impressed Flower most: a national forest campground on Mt. Frazier, about sixty miles north of Los Angeles. The weekend spent here was a prelude to something more; it was filled with beginnings, openings, beckonings; and she left with the feeling that she had touched only its outstretched hand.

Flower camping in the mountains

The opportunity to return to the mountain's serenity and pristine grandeur soon appeared. The couple who had introduced her to Southern California's high country left Los Angeles to manage a motel business in a distant community. In the meantime, her friends Merle and Ruth, seeing the need for assistance in the growth of the work ahead, arranged to share a spacious two story duplex with her family. The fortunate bonus in the deepening of this companionship was a mutual love for the mountains. In May the three set out for an entire month's stay at the Mt. Frazier campsite.

From the beginning it was an idyllic retreat. They spent the pleasant, clear days in study and meditation, interspersed with happy conversation and long, slow walks through the lovely stands of pine and cedar. Not far from their camp was an unusually beautiful grove of tall Jeffrey pines formed in a natural circle. Flower came into their secluded stillness each day to meditate, look out upon the distant horizons, and attune herself to the frequencies of nature. She called this grove the Garden of Trees and one in particular, The Giving Tree, was her choice to sit by. Of all the Jeffrey pines in the vicinity,

65

this one's aura was the most surcharged and outshining; in the height of its branches, presiding over the surrounding region, stood a great deva.

One day, about halfway through the month, Flower was sitting at the foot of this lofty tree, peacefully meditating on the Christ, with no particular expectation in mind, when she heard the sound of approaching footsteps. Wondering who might be coming, she half arose for a clearer view. What she saw made every

The Giving Tree

atom of her body race with whirlwind speed. Through the trees, partially hidden by branches at times, came the unmistakable figure of The Lord Christ. Many times she had seen His higher form in the inner worlds, leading the procession in his honor on Christmas Eve. But this manifestation seemed physical: a condition she had last observed nineteen centuries earlier in Palestine.

He came now into full view and stood in tall nobility, directly in front of her. Had she forgotten the strength of His build? And His dark brown eyes—what equaled their power to engulf one with the love He alone radiated? As He breathed, the white robe He was wearing moved gently. The same breeze that touched her hair, softly stirred His. She was speechless, puzzled by what was happening, and strangely timid. She felt acutely aware of His absolute Presence, an impression that intensified what followed.

He stood there, His gaze penetrating every particle of her being. Then He softly spoke the command: "Be still. Be still."

A sequence of momentous events rushed through her, recreating all of her previous initiations. Joining the Christ now were the Maha Chohan, known as the Holy Spirit, the Kindel Archangel responsible for her life disc, her Guardian, and the Master John.

In the cells of her body she felt a new and tremendous acceleration. This, she now realized, was still another initiation. The impact of its velocities shook her with hurricane intensity; she felt rent asunder, then totally reconstructed by the forces sweeping through her body. Every aspect of this illumination far exceeded anything she had known through clairvoyance alone. Her consciousness was lifted into realms of unguessed luminosity; the tiniest details stood out in sharp relief, and the onrush of the forces pulsing from the atmosphere into the gates of her being surpassed all previous feeling.

She became keenly aware of the *future* and all it promised, *if only she could be true*. Possibility after possibility passed before her eyes, each necessitating for its attainment the pledge of her uncompromising, fearless self-giving.

Precisely this vision of the future, and the need for her whole-hearted commitment to its potentialities, distinguished the initiatory experience from the perceptions of clairvoyance. Without this transcendent incentive, one by one, the flaming opportunities might easily fade like fleeting, unreachable dreams. She had come the long way of evolution not to dream, but to do—that was her charge, perilous in its risks but a prize of unsurpassable worth at journey's end.

With these impressions still blazing in the forge of her memory, the Lord Christ conferred the initiatory degree and confirmed her promises to its monumental commission.

He then addressed her. She remained motionless, listening intently, asking no questions. He spoke of her mission:

she came to help humanity become more aware of the Angel Kingdom and to prepare individuals for higher unfoldment. She wouldn't be a teacher of the masses; instead, her work would be with the more advanced souls, preparing them also to become teachers. He knew the deep disappointment attached to this restriction. Her love for humanity was all-encompassing; she had wished to reach out to the great numbers of people everywhere, longing to see their spiritual fires rekindled. But He encouraged her not to feel burdened by this containment: there would be compensations and companionings to outweigh whatever disappointment she felt.

He said she would need to go into the cities to build up her work, making contacts with the various leaders of metaphysical and esoteric groups in advance; eventually, she would be shown property in a chosen location where this work would have its center. As He completed these statements, one thought filled her: *trust in this wisdom!*

From the moment she first marveled at His presence before the Lord Christ's Giving Tree, time ceased to exist. As He returned to His duties in the inner worlds, leaving her hushed in the lingering vibrations of this ineffable occurrence, she wondered how long it had lasted. The shadows underneath the trees had moved only slightly; though it seemed an eternity, the experience she would cherish as the highest of her incarnation was perhaps twenty minutes in length.

Just looking into His eyes had given her consciousness celestial openings eclipsing all past understanding. It was a baptism of such immensity, its essences perpetually, luminously implanted in the skies of her memory; that throughout her life it would shed warmth and light like an interior sun.

She looked out over the slope of the mountain; its inner light was incredibly pure and crystalline. She sat for hours, steeping herself in the mystical energies clinging magnetically to every particle in the air and each bristling cluster of needles on the Giving Tree. The love she felt for this Jeffrey pine was no less than for a beloved pet and she embraced it with the same outflow of compassion.

Her mind returned again and again to the climactic decisions she had made. The view beyond the mountains was of a large valley far below with a winding road leading down and across its expanse. She heard herself saying, "But I must descend the mountain, go back to the plains of uninspired existence and busy myself in the environment of the city. Otherwise," she mused "the value of what has happened would come to naught."

The thought of leaving this place and returning to the everyday world nearly tore her in two. In that moment it seemed impossible. Down there, she had no mountain of renewal, not even with her clairvoyance. Had it not been necessary for her to venture all the way up to the high altitudes of this holy place, to spend days in unknowing preparation, becoming impregnated with its peace? Then to leave it indefinitely?

But there was a greater challenge whose somber prospect hung uncertainly over her future. The initiatory degree she had taken was a sacrificial one, though no clue had been given of its form or timetable. She now must learn to live with its portentous question, fearlessly holding to God awareness, awaiting the confrontation with whatever must be, wherever it lurked, all with a willing heart.

The solemn tones of these heavier reflections vanished the moment she recalled the transfiguring splendor of the Christ's eyes. No matter what lay ahead, to recapture again their power assured the overcoming of any obstacle, the mastery of every goal. And as precipitous as the mountain of her endeavor seemed, overleaping its steepness was his victorious assurance that *it could be done.*

When it came to her how the hours must have passed, she stood up and reluctantly slipped out of the pine grove, return-

Flower Sechler in 1932

CHAPTER SIX - FLOWER'S MISSION RECEIVED

ing slowly, blissfully to the camp and her two waiting companions. Upon seeing her approach, they knew something remarkable had occurred—her clothes were actually shining. Flower smiled, her face confirming what their glances had sensed. She said nothing, not then or for days to come. She wanted to keep the afterglow intact as long as possible and her friends, she knew, would understand.

When at last the time came to leave, the immanence of this ordeal brought a crisis. To carry out the charge of her initiation she had to reach the highest of conscious states. All at once she had the feeling of being unable to do what had to be done: to return to the plains of the world below and be the wayshower called for by her commission. They were packed and ready to leave but no matter how she tried, her consciousness fell short of the essential threshold.

She went up into the pines one last time, struggling for a breakthrough, but without success. Then, crestfallen, she turned away.

"God knows I've tried," she softly answered herself, "and now I'll have to leave it in His hands."

With the sounding of that sentence, it *came*, flooding over her as before: all jubilant and glorious, pouring through her in a sweet torrent of incandescence. And that was her lesson: not to rely so heavily on herself, but to give it into God's keeping. Her confidence regained, she reaffirmed her promise to bring through *everything* received. But to have left the mountain unsure of her strength, unable to see the way clear to keep her all-encompassing pledge in the face of impending failure, that would have fallen upon her shoulders like a great stone.

The mantling of light surrounded Flower for over a month. Its bestowal made clear the plan of her mission and gave her the impetus to see it through. There was still a further gift: from this time on the mountains would be her inner temples; they would lead to the courts of renewal and empowerment as no other earthly environment provided. She would come back many more times to Mt. Frazier and her beloved Giving Tree. But these later visitations, quickening in their currents, were anticlimactic, never equaling the zenith of her initiatory sunburst.

One return, standing out from the others, did occur the following year when she again spent the month of May at Frazier Park, this time with high expectations. Still, the entire month passed without an unusual incident. When it was time to depart, to ease her disappointment, she felt the need to make one last visit to a favorite viewpoint. Walking up to an area near a redwood reservoir, she stood looking out over the grand panorama of mountains and valleys. Even though nothing memorable had happened, she felt an overflowing gratitude for all that this forested wilderness meant. In that instant, the landscape burst into a shower of light—every rock and growing thing was aglow in a sparkling brilliance. Through this glistening sheen swept a current of Divinity, unfamiliar, yet caressing her with its updrafts of spiritual vitality. Then a space in the inner worlds parted—before her were arrayed the new directions of conquest and what must be done to achieve each. Everything was clear, direct, calling her toward the goal, and with it, the certainty again that *all could be done*!

Around and about shimmered a sea of golden light, vibrantly alive with movement. In the midst of this experience, she returned to the car still rapt in its undiminished splendors. For one of her companions the brightness surrounding her was too strong to look upon comfortably. All the way down the mountain it fed her. Merle and Ruth had tears in their eyes, so visible was the ecstasy on Flower's face. Even when she arrived home, breaking the silence, its energies clung like charged particles. It was more than a month before the last of its endowment faded.

Chapter 7

Lawrence and Questhaven

The two years at Mt. Frazier, like a magnificent summit and a lesser peak beneath, marked the boundary between the shorelands of preparation and the unchartered interior of the continent she had come to colonize. Merle, in her off duty time as a nurse, acted as Flower's secretary, writing letters of inquiry wherever addresses of metaphysical and Truth groups could be found. She now was speaking regularly as far north as San Francisco and south to Long Beach, continuing her commitments in Santa Barbara and the several Unity and New Thought centers in and around Los Angeles.

The swift pace of this activity made the months scatter like leaves before a brisk wind. It was a time of joyous, whole-hearted adventuring: meeting new people, traveling to new places, breaking new ground in the highlands of her spiritual authority: *esoteric Christian mysticism*. The time was drawing near, she knew, to speak the word beyond California and begin publishing her experiences and teachings. Expectantly, she waited to see how this would come about.

The next city to answer an inquiry from her secretary was San Bernardino, a community some fifty miles east of Los Angeles on the edge of the Mojave Desert. Her Guardian promised an unusual surprise was in the making and a date was set for an address at its Unity Center. One of its patrons, who owned an imposing mansion nearby, invited Flower to be a house guest during her stay. When she arrived, however, there was a change of plans. It was May, 1933, two months after the disastrous Long Beach earthquake and the intended host had been called away to look after damaged property.

One of the women at the Center, whose home was large and comfortable, heard of this plight and volunteered to have Flower as a guest, driving her there that afternoon. Staying in the house as its lone roomer was a young man with dark hair, large, shining eyes and a radiant smile.

In return for a portion of his board, he was about his weekly task of mowing the lawn when they pulled up to the curb.

As soon as she stepped out of the car, they looked into each others' eyes and a flash of recognition swept through them. Dropping the handle of the lawnmower, he rushed over to help with the luggage, the hostess introducing him simply as "Lawrence Newhouse, my roomer."

Lawrence George Newhouse

All the while, Flower's eyes never ceased gazing into his. The sheer surprise of the encounter caught her in silent fascination. Neither her guardian nor the Teachers of Life had foretold such a meeting, yet the reassurances of help and companioning received at Mt. Frazier suddenly manifested in the light of his wondering face. Lawrence, a close companion of many lives, marvelously standing there, his outstretched hand clasping hers. Her heart danced to see, glistening in his eyes, the reflection of the same fascination.

Flower spoke next, a hopeful invitation in her voice:

"Will you be coming to my lecture tonight?"

"Yes, of course I will," he answered, as if confirming a long-standing intention.

When she was escorted to her room and he had returned reluctantly to finish the lawn, the hostess slipped back into the room excitedly. Lawrence, she confided, had never planned to go to the lecture at all. In fact, when she had asked him to come with her to hear "a very interesting guest speaker," he declined, remembering his duties at a Masonic temple meeting that same night. "You must have made quite an impression," the woman laughed teasingly.

That night, as Flower spoke on the subject of the Angel Kingdom, a mist lifted, bringing to life for Lawrence a world bursting with unguessed marvels. But what he heard was the lesser impression—the one upon whom he looked, and who looked back joyously at him, what could compare to the torrent of gladness her face sent cascading through his heart? He knew, as she knew, what the future held.

Their courtship grew as naturally as a garden blooms from the roots and seeds of another year. Though Lawrence immediately realized their oneness, he had no memory of the past; she, however, remembered him from Peru, Egypt, and Palestine: three lives in which they knew each other as pupils, though never before as husband and wife. He had no preparation in the present incarnation for the mystery teachings or the gifts of clairvoyance, yet he accepted both as easily as a sailor welcomes the sight of land after a long voyage on the open sea. His intuition, seasoned from past training, quickly grasped their validity. Hastening these recognitions were his beloved's reality and beauty before him—not that love dissolved any reservations he otherwise might have felt; love, instead, stirred the quiescent coals of his memory so long banked in the ashes of unconsciousness. Like fresh flames leaping up to illuminate the world about him, dormant remembrances, one by one, took their places in a growing light, reinstating the scheme of things once familiar long ago.

The orbit of Lawrence's life now altered its course sharply. Five years earlier, he had left his birthplace in Franklin Park, Illinois, a suburb of Chicago, venturing west as a high school graduation present from his parents. California captured his imagination: it seethed with possibilities and drew him irresistibly across the threshold of his future.

He needed a job. With an invisible purposefulness, the friends with whom he was staying arranged a position in the printing firm where the husband was employed. It was a profession that suited Lawrence's appreciation of excellence and by the end of his third year in California he was well along the way to becoming a master craftsman.

When Flower inquired about his work, the answer thrilled her: she hadn't needed further confirmation of the destiny behind their meeting, but the fitting together of his vocation with her desire to write fell in place like an exclamation point.

The weekend in San Bernardino was a turning point for both Flower and Lawrence Their time together was too brief and the vast numbers of things two people wish to know about each other when falling so swiftly, wholly in love, scarcely were tapped. She was scheduled for a month of lectures in San Francisco and characteristically saw this as an opportunity for both of them to test the true nature of their feelings toward one another. Yet the only trial of this separation was the painful longing to be in each other's presence once more: no fleeting doubts or second thoughts arose.

Both had previously met persons about whom they cared and even contemplated marriage. Now these possibilities dissolved. What happened on that afternoon when they

Flower A. Newhouse in 1934

first came together was such a bright finding, no one else could be seen against its radiance. Whether together or apart, it simply grew greater—though being together was its hearth fire and apartness was like stepping out into the elements on a lonely errand, already looking forward to the warmth and cheer of the return.

When the month was up, so was their endurance. As often as possible now, Lawrence found his way into Los Angeles and her home. It was clear not only to them, but to everyone who saw them together, this was a love of boundless magnitude.

Flower's mother, alone, resisted its prospect. Her daughter had become the foundation of her personal security. Marriage to her meant some young man, however nice, spiriting away a part of herself, and she was unable to overcome the mounting fear that she was about to lose her daughter, not gain a son.

Perhaps Lawrence's irrepressible optimism and gladness reminded her, in some strange way, of her last husband's extravagant disposition and flamboyant promises, none of which came to any good. But between Flower and Lawrence fell the shadow of her mother's obsessive insecurity. When any discussion of marriage was broached, there were peculiar reactions: complaints, criticisms, a change of subject—and as the likelihood of this union increased, "heart pains" and fainting spells.

Flower knew her mother too well to misread these symptoms. She had freed Flower in every important way, following her inner promptings when they mattered most, until now. It made no difference that there was every reason to expect the opposite of her fears. The threat was too entangled in the roots of her anxiety to overcome or ignore.

One thing was clear to Flower: she mustn't let her mother keep them apart. She wished not to hurt her, but simultaneously recognized what was at stake if she yielded in her favor. It must be settled now, decisively marking the boundary between her mother's life and her own.

The solution was both considerate and immutable: on All Saints Eve, October 31, 1933, they were secretly married. It was a plan thoughtfully bridging the chasm of the mother's fears by granting one concession: they would not, for the present, live together as husband and wife. Neither would there exist any battleground on which to dispute the issue of marriage.

The farsightedness of this decision proved worth the price of a temporary separation. By the time her mother finally learned of the irrevocable fact, it was too late to block it. The realization, too, that she was a mother-in-law of several months standing eased her across an otherwise impassable threshold. Lawrence's great kindliness and attention as a son-in-law accomplished the rest. On April 28, 1934, this time with her mother, sister, and friends in attendance, a second ceremony was held at Forest Lawn's Wee Kirk of the Heather in Glendale.

Flower and Lawrence Newhouse in 1934

Marriage and its spiritual partnership marked the final step of preparation for the mission entrusted to Flower. Her life, though presenting many surprises and unforeseeable turns, obediently flowed through the channels long ago encoded in her life disc and reexperienced during the initiation on Mt. Frazier. She had only *to be true* and all things would come about.

A small booklet called *The School of Life*, written four years earlier, was now published through a friend in Santa Barbara. It had come to her in an updraft of inspiration to explain in simple, direct words, the mysteries and purpose of life. Two of Flower's distinguishing characteristics were, as a teacher, clarity, and as a mystic, practicality. In this book both qualities mingled congenially as she drew the analogy between one's progress in school and evolution's goal of Mastery through successive incarnations. The power of her writing emerged in the contrast between the simplicity of her words and the fathomless complexity of her grasp of truth. It was the enigma of her genius: to speak plainly of incalculable immensities, pointing first to the branches of the Tree of Life within reach. She was a pioneer of spiritual mathematics, writing a concise overview of the arithmetic of beginning discipleship.

Still, between writing and speaking, it was the latter that would dominate her career, win the permanence of a following, and reveal the most facets of her reality. Writing lacked the spontaneity and visible contact with its audience that speaking afforded. Writing was suited more for the activities of reflection and revision whereas speaking drew its strength from the inspirations and intuitions streaming through the world of spirit, responsive to the subtle uniqueness of each situation, each group.

To see her, to look into her eyes, to experience first-hand the light in her face—and then to hear the melodious flow of

Flower A. Newhouse in 1936

her words: rising in gladness, brimming with love, vibrant with wonder, measuring out truths with fearless authority—these were the unforgettable impressions of those who heard her.

It was not simply her command of esoteric knowledge, nor even her clairvoyance that won souls to her cause. It was her astonishing embodiment of Christ-like qualities that caught them unaware. Those who came merely to collect an interesting idea or novel viewpoint, left with a flaming vision of one of Christ's messengers emblazoned in their memories. In place of an idea, shone the image of a living person enkindling the embers of a mysterious kinship. Something from long ago and far away stirred within them—but more than that, there was a premonition, a sense of what the future promised, if only they could find the way and keep true.

Lawrence now entered into her work with equal energy, every day awakening more fully to the Cause she stood for. They lived in Los Angeles one month, then moved to Glendora where he found a job on a small newspaper. His wages were twenty dollars a week and under the meticulous scrutiny of the owner, a staunch taskmaster of Mormon faith, he quickly became expert in all phases of printing.

But the principal activity their marriage made possible, the one most vital to the founding of what was now their ministry, was *speaking the word*. Arrangements were made to spend six months of every second year touring the nation, lecturing wherever her Guardian prompted them to go. Lawrence's employer was agreeable to this schedule, the nature of his business being sufficiently seasonal to allow it, and their work leaped forward.

The first tour was made in Lawrence's little two-seater Ford coupe with a rolldown top, crossing the United States. It never failed to get them from one destination to the next, but during the winter months it was drafty and cold; they had to bundle up with blankets, wrapping them tight about their ears to keep out the frosty air.

The essential practice on these tours, a discipline she had learned long before meeting Lawrence, was the exercise of faith, on their own, to make the way clear: faith enough for provision, for new opportunities, and for the know-how to deal with the unpredictable mixture of groups. These ranged from persons, in some instances, with orthodox backgrounds through those acquainted with the teachings of such metaphysical and esoteric movements as Religious Science, Unity, Theosophy, and the Rosicrucians. Some were coldly intellectual and critical; others were envious of her incomparable attainments. But most of those who came to a lecture were deeply touched by her message and, multiplying its validity, her presence—these were the ones who passed through the archway of readiness into the temple of her teachings. They consumed every word in a great thirst for each pristine revelation, never before having heard the first person descriptions or fresh pronouncements of a living mystic. Some, perhaps only one or two in an audience, if at all, were at the melting point of discipleship where they awakened to her true identity: more than a lecturer or seer—a wayshower. For these began an abrupt and transcendent odyssey out of the wastelands of Everyday toward the distant Himalayas of inner reality.

Slowly, a nucleus of individuals stepped forward in one city, then another, asking the salient question: "How do I keep in touch with you; how can I become your pupil?"

At first glance, Flower's answer was simple enough: to write them at their Glendora address and to send for the Inspiration Letter, soon to be published. She then shared with them a promise for the future: she and Lawrence were looking for property where, one day, they would establish a center. At that time, God and the pupil willing, they should make plans to move west and help pioneer this enterprise.

In the next five years, Flower and Lawrence visited 105 cities in the United States and two in Canada. She conducted several retreats at Mt. Frazier and initiated a series of annual pilgrimages in Medford, Oregon, where a sizable following had grown. From their home in Glendora, she personally answered the hundreds of letters that now arrived, each tour adding to the harvest.

Finances on these tours, while their most practical test, became inexhaustible demonstrations of Divine ingenuity. They seldom set out with more than twenty dollars between them, on tours that would span the country, taking them as far north as Canada. They would be gone for months with nothing to fall back on but their Olympian trust in the passkey of faith.

It was not unusual to arrive in a city having spent all of their funds covering the previous day's expenses: meals, lodging, hall rental, newspaper notices, and gas for the car. They were never apprehensive or disquieted; they knew the love offering that night would be sufficient to settle their immediate costs or, waiting for them, possibly an invitation to be someone's guests overnight. If the collection at one engagement fell short it was often balanced by an overgenerous offering at another. Total strangers would slip five and ten dollar bills into their hands without a word of need having been mentioned. In one form or another, as the pool of their supply emptied itself at one end it was filled at the other. And this became Flower's archetype for finances throughout their lives: an open pool, flowing freely, forever refilling and freshening itself.

More and more, the immanence of finding property for a headquarters invaded their attention. The question and answer period following tour lectures brought many inquiries about future plans and the answer seemed always to begin: "Someday, when we have our center...."

Already they had searched out a number of locations along the west coast as far north as Oregon and Washington. More and more, however, Flower realized it would be California—probably within the southern half of the state. The strip of land stretching about fifty miles inland between the border of Mexico, north to San Luis Obispo, she had been instructed, was the cradle of the New Age. Santa Barbara interested them and every visit to this charming city included time for property hunting. But several years had passed in this search and their dream of a spacious piece of land ideally suitable for retreat purposes seemed no closer.

They began spending weekends pursuing any lead or intuition coming to them; by the early part of 1940 there were few areas left in Southern California that they had not scouted thoroughly.

Then one Sunday morning while having an early breakfast, they came upon an intriguing ad in the Los Angeles Times announcing the availability of a 440-acre tract in northern San Diego County. It was the first appearance of this particular notice and they both were strongly drawn to its investigation. With the realtor's phone number, Flower's mother and a friend visiting them from Oregon, they headed south to the adobe and granite hills hiding the quaint little community of Vista.

The countryside about them was lovely and green following the abundant winter rains; predominantly low rolling hills clustered with avocado and citrus groves. After picking up the woman realtor and driving farther south into a remote region of picturesque hills, she listed some of the virtues of the property they were about to see. It lay right in the middle of what the local Chamber of Commerce called the "perfect climate belt:" an area just inland from the coast averaging, throughout the year, the least temperature variation in the nation. Its highest point overlooked the Pacific ocean, about eight miles to the west; mild coastal winds cooled it in the summer and made the wintertime pleasant. And, she added, with a little fixing up, there was a rustic stone cottage just waiting for someone to move in.

They turned off the last of the paved highways and continued along a winding country road for about three and a half miles. By now they were in a completely isolated range of hills with nothing to remind them of the outside world except each other, their car, and the dirt road rising to the summit of a ridge just ahead. Reaching this point, their guide asked Lawrence to pull off the side, just as the road turned down steeply into a large, wooded canyon.

"That's the property over there," she said, pointing off in the direction of a small house tucked away along a distant slope on the far side of the valley.

Flower's heart sang. There was no doubt: this was the end of their search; they had found their center. It lay below them peacefully, like a Shangri-la waiting secretly behind a mountain rim. Slowly her eyes drank from the pool of its beauty. Stands of native oak traced the wandering course of a stream bed through the length of the canyon. A lush forest of coastal chaparral covered everything in sight, giving the entire setting an evergreen luxuriance. Three or four birds soared gracefully back and forth across the expanse and a rabbit dashed to the edge of a thicket, then turned to regard them curiously.

Flower looked at Lawrence and reached for his hand, her eyes saying, *yes! . . . yes!*

The realtor pointed to a grove of olive trees half sub-

Questhaven around 1946

85

merged in the overgrowth of chaparral below and off to one side of the house. They had been planted, she explained, around the turn of the century by some German immigrants who hoped to establish productive orchards, then abandoned them for lack of water. But the strong-hearted, drought-resistant trees still survived.

Flower's eye caught the rows of silver-green trees lying like patchwork across an otherwise virgin hillside—how strange that this land so long promised, so quietly waiting for them, would have this link with Palestine and Greece: a tree going back to the meeting places of her two most memorable incarnations.

Eagerly they returned to the car and made their way down into the canyon. On every side, something delightful greeted them, as if primed for the celebration of this moment. Coveys of quail, in a spirited quickstep, scurried off into the underbrush. Lovely groves of oak invited their eyes along pathways beneath a lacy tangle of foliage. When the car came around a corner upon a setting of trees filtering the soft sunlight onto the bright green leaves of the undergrowth, a melodious brook splashed across the road, picking up its stream bed on the other side, meandering off in a sparkling ribbon of clear water.

The car pulled out into an opening at the edge of the oaks and turned up a narrow entrance road leading to the house. It was situated in a clearing on a hillside, surrounded by a sloping field of wild grass and clumps of native shrubs. Its walls, the realtor observed, were made of stone quarried on the site and a broad porch welcomed its visitors, offering a far-reaching view of the horizon.

It was badly run down and in need of repair, but as Flower and Lawrence walked through its three rooms, their imagination transformed it into a charming, cozy dwelling. There was a spacious living room with a large fireplace, a small but adequate kitchen, and the bedroom with a tiny bath to one side. Upstairs, by way of a narrow staircase, they found an unfinished attic suitable for storage or a future guest room, and underneath the house was a crude earthen basement cut into the hard granite hillside.

The entire structure was rough, and though quite solid, confessed the telltale handiwork of a conscientious amateur. One corner of the ceiling in the living room was stained with large brown splotches and sagged from the weight of a mysterious substance oozing through the plaster; on closer inspection it turned out to be honey. The realtor explained that the only use given the property in recent years was as a bee-keeping range and the house was an inviting refuge for stray swarms of these industrious creatures.

Blue Gables in 1940, built around 1890

Lawrence inquired about the previous owner and Flower's eyes widened at the answer: a husband and wife by the name of Richard and Isabella Ingalese had purchased the grounds in 1919, 21 years earlier, planning to establish a center for their own spiritual work. She knew him as a teacher and writer in the field of the New Thought movement. Wasn't it curious that he, too, saw in these hills the destiny she and Lawrence beheld? When ill health and death in 1935 finally brought an end to his dream, the title changed hands and drifted into another estate settlement, leading to the ad in the Los Angeles Times.

This brought them to the fateful question: how much were they asking for the house and the 440 acres? Lawrence already had formulated a second question in the back of his mind, since so many acres likely were well beyond their financial resources: would they sell the house and part of the land?

The realtor's reply came as a pleasant surprise: "Forty-two hundred and fifty dollars."

Still, as attractive as the price sounded, to Lawrence it might as well have been ten times that amount; he looked questioningly at Flower. Her face shone with confidence—not a trace of perplexity or hesitation.

"How much of a down payment would that require?" she asked.

Lawrence was delighted. Knowing the irrepressible fortitude of his wife's faith, he swallowed his second question. And why not the entire property? It was a piece of unplundered creation, reaching beyond the horizon of sheltering hills to the east and west—a place where one could come in the midst of its peace to find God. In its isolation and stillness, it closed a door to one world, opening onto another. For one who was aware, even the air was alive with the breath of Divinity and every growing thing quivered with the pulse of Eternity's heartbeat.

The question of the down payment began an encouraging discussion that swept clean the last corner of doubt. As they walked outdoors to look about the countryside, both Flower and Lawrence knew in that moment it belonged to them, and through their mission, to Christ.

The ground was soft from the recent rains and as they walked from one point to another, they felt the tenderness of the land yielding underfoot, its mothering surge to life visible in the delicate grasses and sprouting bulbs of spring flowers whose leafy shoots cushioned every step.

From a vista high on a ridge overlooking the central area, a gentle Pacific wind cooled their faces. How near to God this day had brought them. Even the hills seemed to kneel in worship, hushed before His Presence.

Returning to the car, they took one last look about. There was no electricity and the nearest telephone was in Vista, nine miles to the north. A dry, abandoned well meant that a dependable supply of water was yet to be developed. In every way, the life awaiting them was a pioneer's. To Lawrence it promised high adventure and a bright, harvest-filled future. To Flower it was her mission's citadel: the holy ground of her pilgrimage and the soil where she would plant the seedling of the Tree of Life entrusted to her.

"And its name—" a friend asked as they drove down a few weeks later to complete the purchase arrangements, "what will you call your retreat?"

Flower thought a moment. "It should have 'quest' in its name," she said, "for that will be its purpose, and it should be a 'haven' to all who come."

"That's it," exclaimed their friend, "Quest Haven."

Chapter 8

The Years of Pioneering

For Flower and Lawrence 1940 became a year of weekends. All of their savings went into the down payment along with gifts from their friends responding to a joyous appeal for funds as the word of Quest Haven's finding was broadcast. From Monday through Friday, Lawrence at the Glendora Press and Flower writing and lecturing, they worked to spread the Word and gather in every penny toward the day the property would be debt free and they could live and support themselves on its grounds.

On Friday evening, they would load food and blankets in their car, then head south to their hill-hidden sanctuary. As each mile fell behind them the pull of man's world eased and the sense of God's world quickened. A final hill, a last turn, and once more they were there.

Finding Quest Haven was a turning point that sharply separated past from future. All that preceded it was prologue—her reawakening to the inner worlds, the instruction by her Guardian, the unfoldment of her teaching skills, their marriage, and Lawrence's readiness to serve the Cause with her. Now began a joint enterprise: building a center dedicated to the

Early Sign

91

Christ, His mystery teachings, His *way* to God. Before, they were as wayfarers in a strange land, seeking out kinsmen for a homeland concealed behind the veil of time, and now the veil had lifted. Like spirit joining flesh, Flower and Lawrence planted their hearts in the virgin earth of Quest Haven and a fresh, living essence came into being.

First to be transformed was the stone cottage. Flower's Pennsylvania Dutch upbringing was more than a match for its long-neglected cupboards and floors. Each weekend wit-

Flower waving from a replenished house

nessed a scouring and scrubbing that would have won the smiling approval of her most immaculate aunt back in Allentown. Flower loved making things shining clean. Every polished ledge and dusted corner paralleled the way of discipleship. This was the oneness of life on all levels: homes must be clean and neatly kept, also bodies and emotions, habits and motives, feelings and thoughts. One without the others meant a lack of wholeness and until each level of one's existence mirrored the purity of its Creator, life's lessons remained unfinished.

And as she worked she sang—lilting, melodious airs of this world and that of her nativity, just as she had done while a pupil in the school of Pythagoras.

A visitor helping her could only be impressed by her joy in these tasks. Whatever is there to sing about? might run their thoughts—it is a job that must be done, that's all, but to burst forth into song! To be thrilled with work! What kind of a person would do such a thing?

Flower cleaned with more than her hands and knees; she cleaned with love. The unconventional way she dusted and scrubbed was arresting: she treated the scrub brush quite like a valued possession, with tenderness and care, not abusing it as something to get an unpleasant job out of the way. A dust cloth was folded with the same consideration as an article of clothing being tucked away in a drawer. She stroked a window sill or a pane of glass gently, over and over, revealing all of its hidden luster.

The same visitor might wonder why she bothered being so thorough about her housekeeping; there were so many other duties more deserving of her time and attention. If they asked the question, or insisted on relieving her, she would say, "But I love doing this, don't you? It's good for me to do these things."

Lawrence undertook the multitude of repairs and improvements about the house with good-natured pleasure. There was the matter of the honey above the living room ceiling, some broken windows, rusted screens, a new roof, the laying of linoleum, and, with Flower joining in, painting inside and out.

As the months passed the little building changed from its drab, run-down appearance to a warm, charming cottage. Gaily colored curtains, polished brass kerosene lamps, bouquets of fresh flowers, a soft rug before two Early California arm chairs, and the appetizing smell of a succulent dinner permeating the interior, all became part of its new atmosphere.

Water, which at first they carried in cans and bottles to meet their weekend needs, was provided by a deeper well equipped with a sturdy new windmill that pumped cool water into a small concrete reservoir above their home. This development opened the way for a garden, landscaping, and their favorite project, tree planting. Carefully they selected

93

Early windmill to provide water

a variety of trees: Australian eucalyptus for their graceful lines and hardy disposition; a line of Idaho locust on either side of a road leading up to a lovely clearing dominated by a magnificent oak tree; shamel ash, acacia, jacaranda, liquidambar, ginkgo, and pepper trees added to this array, along with fruit trees: avocado, navel and valencia oranges, dwarf lemon, fig, and loquat. And in greatest profusion, evergreens: Monterey, Torrey, and Tamarack pine, Himalayan deodar and incense cedar, Canary Island and yellow pine, and hosts of others. These, representing the most highly evolved of earth's species, were her favorite trees. They drew power from the nature world that no other trees commanded, attracting deva presences and other beings of great benefit to the inner beauty of the countryside.

To give the trees the start they needed meant carrying buckets full of water often hundreds of yards; in one instance, a half mile up a steep trail to one of the highest points on the property. Sometimes Flower insisted on carrying the heavy buckets over the rough ground and up the rugged slopes, happily setting aside Lawrence's admonitions to the contrary. She would laugh and say, "Now, Lawrence, it's all right. I'll take several rests."

When at last they reached a promising location, he would dig a large basin, cut open the container, and, setting the tree's roots into the soft earth, watch the pure delight on his beloved's face as she poured the cool flood

94

of water upon the tree.

Within a year there was sufficient money to pay off the indebtedness of the property and allow Flower and Lawrence to make their permanent residence at the retreat. On the fourth of August, 1940, in the Oak Grove Sanctuary, Flower performed the dedication service. Only a handful of people were present as she spoke of their dream in the years to come when hundreds and perhaps thousands of people someday might gather in study and retreat.

Trees planted and hand watered on Inspiration Point

"The objectives to which the Christward Ministry is pledged," she said, "are fivefold: First, to increase the recognition of the Christ Spirit throughout the earth. Second, to support the great Christ Ministry. Third, to strive for the awakenment of every individual's Christ consciousness. Fourth, to apply the Christ Principles in everyday living. And fifth, to know that there is no end to Christ unfoldment and enlightenment."

She emphasized that Quest Haven was not only to serve the Christ in their lifetime but throughout the centuries to come; how it would attract writers, artists, composers, businessmen, scientists, statesmen, and simply the earnest seeker. There were challenging qualifications: "Every inch of this ground is consecrated to the Christed Jesus."

"Those who visit or work here must in some measure exemplify the Christ consciousness and power in his character and works."

She offered prayers to the Triune Spirit of God and to the

hosts of Angels, one by one, whose interest this retreat would serve. Then came the last, immense consecration: "*And now in the awareness of what we do, we reverently bequeath Quest Haven to the Christ, forever.*"

Flower leading a service in the Oak Grove

That final word cut through the air like a charge of lightning, investing itself deep in the heart of the trees, chaparral-covered hills and the earth itself. In that moment, the auric radiation about Quest Haven changed, its colors brightening and its activity accelerating in tempo. Flower's eyes moved about her, examining these differences and appreciating the permanence of this sacrament. If only everyone present could see for himself how extraordinarily more alive and vibrant were the inner worlds—especially at such a moment of holiness. If she could only share an instant of her clairvoyance with each celebrant, how startlingly beautiful, awesomely reverent their experience would be.

Lawrence now gave full time to printing the Inspiration Letter, a monthly publication going back to 1934, to the care and building of Quest Haven, and to his wife. Their love seemed to belong to another world, beginning like the sudden opening of a gate eight years earlier and growing closer to God as a road approaches the center of a city. But its course was neither easy nor inevitable. Flower came into life with a mission she vowed daily to uphold. It gave no room for rival purposes or divided loyalties. She must either fulfill or fail, and against a thousand ways to fail, there was but a single path to victory: to serve the Cause of Christ above all else—above family, above husband, and most exactingly, above self.

Lawrence, though not consciously able to recall point for point the life rules behind his own incarnation, as could his wife, found them through his intuition and his appreciation of her true reality. He loved her with more than the commonplace love that wishfully projects itself upon another person with a blaze of fervent idealism, only to fade eventually into the ordinary light of reality. He loved her worshipingly, as a wayshower—one who would lead them across the planet of life, and as one wanting to share the hardships and fortunes of losing self in the finding of God. He loved her, too, as a woman whose warmth, tenderness, and joy surpassed human limits, reminding him, over and over, of her origin.

Knowing who she was, and what she had come to do, Lawrence clasped his own life's mission by giving himself utterly to service as her second-in-command. Everything else he relinquished, if he had it to give: personal ambition, ego, pride, envy, self-pity, and the unquenchable pleasures of self-centeredness.

Lawrence holding one of their cats

After a busy day, especially if he had been tried in his work or around other people preoccupied with worldly matters, he would pause at the door to "Blue Gables," as they came to call their home, saying inwardly to himself: "May I be cleansed of all the unholy debris of this day. Purify me that I may be a worthy companion to my sweetheart, in Christ's Service."

Living true to this prayer, he gave to their marriage an uplift that made, for Flower, the vital difference between a single and a double burden. It is one thing to give your life to God—another, to find, on top of that, you must carry a lagging partner through the wearisome struggles of choosing between God one day and self the next. This dilemma never arose.

In being what he was, Lawrence surmounted this most formidable test of his early life, a psychological storm center that a lesser person would have found catastrophic: to dedicate one's love to a marriage, in turn, consigned to God, and not fall victim to a backlash of jealousy toward one's supernatural rival. Another might have regressed to an ineffectual shadow of a man or reacted with explosive, abusive resistance. Lawrence simply set aside his own ego in favor of his Christ Self within, quietly, without dramatization, as if it required nothing more.

Flower with her beloved pets

Rather than resisting or rebelling, Lawrence grew beyond himself into this new nature. And his great example to those grasping its reality was this act of self-transcendence achieved here and now. Flower, who came into life with this attainment complete, shone with the imperial mystery of her conquest where Lawrence, before the eyes of all who knew him, daily walked up the initiatory steps in everything he did, pausing occasionally to smile and catch his breath with some encouraging observation, then move on.

Flower and Lawrence leading an Idyllwild Retreat

About Lawrence there was a radiance that was mystifying in its constancy and authenticity. Its quality was the same whether faced with victory, misfortune, or the plain events of every day. It seemed to say, "Life is a glorious gift—rejoice in it, shine with it, send it into the lives of everyone around you, and in gladness give thanks."

It streamed from his large, dark, luminous eyes and a face that, if not beaming with a smile at the moment, held the promise of one soon to come. Taking a problem to Lawrence, even in these early days, was a solution in itself. The impact of both his great-heartedness and his light-filled spirit dissolved the trouble quickly. Just the realization of his willingness to listen and advise, giving of his scarce time, often made the problem seem trivial or suddenly bearable. But likely as not he'd find a way to make the problem an adventure: a grade to be passed, a black knight to be vanquished, a mountain to be climbed. He was fond of the saying, "The difficult we do right away—the impossible takes a little longer;" it was certainly his own faith's caliber.

Lecture tours held a new meaning now that Quest Haven was established. They approached every audience wondering who might be there that night, on the brink of discovering their spiritual legacy in the persons of Flower and Lawrence and a homeland called Quest Haven.

Flower lecturing at a Retreat

Flower scarcely could restrain herself during the talk, anticipating the question and answer period which she began by announcing the reality of their training and retreat headquarters. Setting up a screen, Lawrence concluded the program showing colored slides of the property with views of their cottage, the Oak Grove Sanctuary, Inspiration Point overlooking the Pacific, the olive groves, and nature trails. He included scenes of their dogs and cats following Flower on walks in the early evening, closeups of native wild flowers, and even shots of their tree planting.

They no longer answered inquiries about the future of their work with hopes and promises: "Quest Haven is dedicated to the Christ for all time to come. Our center always will be there and both my husband and I trust to see you there soon," she proclaimed with her eyes sparkling.

Individuals who felt prompted to ask if she saw them among her following in San Diego County, invariably heard her say, "Oh, yes, I see you there by next summer," or "within two years," or whatever her intuition sensed.

Before long, people began arriving from all parts of the country: from the northwest, the midwest, the east, and the

100

south. Their numbers were few at first, but steady. Week-long annual conclaves had been held at a ranch called "Hilltop" in Medford, Oregon since 1936, drawing students from California, Oregon, Washington, Montana, and Idaho. From this nucleus came numerous families as the onset of World War II, in one of its creative turns, closed down old jobs and opened up new ones, especially in the San Diego area.

By the summer of 1943, the second in a series of annual pilgrimages, as they were now called, was held at the lovely estate of *Aum Haven*, adjacent to the Santa Barbara Botanical Gardens in that city. Of the more than two hundred people in attendance, a third of this number had relocated to new homes, jobs, and schools in communities near Quest Haven in the past year.

Flower spoke with a fresh emphasis and a new, more positive authority. Lessons that in previous years were revelations of the nature and Angel Kingdoms now gave increased attention to discipleship: living the life, following the way—the way of the Christ.

In the content of clairvoyance—inner presences, thought forms, auras, and the unceasing sound, activity, and color comprising the inner worlds—there were dangers: lessons driven home to her as far back as Egypt and Greece. Curiosity, for one thing, was a hazardous, grossly insufficient motive. Clairvoyance was a two-edged sword and underneath the world of Light was one of darkness so invested with evil that for one unprepared to meet its satanic powers, the price was madness. Just to observe a drug addict, an alcoholic, a prostitute, or a psychotic patient from the inner dimensions could tear one's emotional body asunder. Hell, she added, is precisely these horrible states of hopelessness and suffering.

There was a more subtle, spiritually lethal risk to a premature interest in clairvoyance: a fascination with glamour, power, and phenomena. Altogether, these three motives encompassed the dark side of superphysical life known as black magic or sorcery. To use these skills solely to win a following, to exalt one's ego, to exploit the gullible, to feel the intoxicating thrill of an occult force near at hand; that is to risk soul and sanity together.

She illustrated this crossroads with a remarkable story out of her own past. When she was eighteen and speaking to truth students in her Los Angeles home once a week, she was advised by a friend that a minister, terribly crippled with arthritis, wanted to attend the next lecture but his affliction had so misshapen his body she should be prepared against a shock.

The evening of the lecture arrived and at its conclusion she went to the rear of the room to greet him. As she approached, she drew back with a muffled gasp. What repulsed her wasn't his physical appearance but his inner identity which suddenly manifested. He had been the leader of the rebellious Egyptian priests during her life in the Temples of Amenhotep IV—a man whose cruel ambitions sent large numbers of priests and priestesses to their deaths in dungeons and torture chambers. One realization eased the horror of seeing him again: the agony embedded in the lines of his face and the twisted purgatory of his body. He could barely lift his head high enough to look into her eyes and he spoke haltingly through his pain. After they exchanged greetings, he looked at Flower with tears brimming in his eyes as he said, "I see you remember me, Meriamen."

Hearing her Egyptian name from this man's lips after more than three and a half millenniums, spoken now without malice, loosened a wave of compassion for his plight. Deliberately, humbly, he began reviewing his circumstances since that time. He wanted her to know he had suffered mercilessly in this and his previous life. He now had no dependable way of earning money and his only income was from the sale of small religious tracts he wrote along esoteric lines. For most of his life he had no knowledge of God's reason for giving him the cross of this body to bear but he knew its purpose was profoundly significant. He traveled as much as he could and on nights that he lacked money for lodging he went to the local jail, asking permission to stay as their guest for the night. He would be fed and allowed to sleep in an unlocked cell. Then one evening the jailer, instead of sympathizing with his request, treated him as a prisoner, pushing him into a cell and slamming the door fast behind him. He fell to the floor, stunned by this mistreatment, and as he struggled to get back to his feet visions of his life as the temple priest passed before him. He saw all of his heinous acts, one by one, relived. The mystery of his arthritis vanished as he saw the people he condemned disappear into narrow underground cells, dripping with foul-smelling water, where their bodies slowly were contorted with the same infirmity inflicted upon him.

When they parted that evening, he begged her to use his example to warn others of evil's inescapable hold on the individual grasping its powers, catching up with them in future incarnations like the descent of an ancient curse.

The story had its happier side, too: the promise of a great debt paid and of a man, struggling to become whole again, on whom the lesson of error and its inexorable consequences were imprinted for the remainder of his evolution.

In the beginning, as in the end, the disciple's first task is the achievement of character, she emphasized. Only then can the gates to the inner worlds open safely and beneficially. To press this fact home, she recalled the unsparing disciplines of her training in the mystery schools of Ikhnaton, Pythagoras and The Christ. In Pythagoras' school alone a full ten years of preparation was given entirely to acquiring self-conquest, holy obedience, and tuning of the instrument. Even then, out of many aspirants, only a handful of candidates met the criteria for the unobstructed unfoldment of their superphysical faculties.

Her message aimed at a simple realization: do not be impatient to possess the gift of clairvoyance—only aspire to serve God by preparing yourself to be a worthy pupil.

How she was what she taught! Standing there, her face was shining with the earned authority that rises from the fires of an interior sun evolved over lifetimes. What she asked of others, she possessed. She was, astonishingly, a realist—she didn't speak of the unfolded life in idealistic or visionary terms, but as realities within reach of everyone. Nor was her mysticism unfathomable or wrapped in obscure abstractions. It was, first of all, the immediate, direct perception of God through extended consciousness progressively revealing the actuality of the inner worlds. What one awakened to was no projection of unconscious dynamisms or imaginings, as so often is the case, but a vast universe of creation as independent of the observer as the galaxies glimpsed by a telescope, and as revolutionary in its impact on consciousness as the discovery of these galaxies to modern astronomers. In a word, one's view of the self and the scheme of things becomes irreversibly transformed.

She was also practical. Her approach to discipleship tirelessly searched for ways to make growth happen. Examples, techniques, illustrations from real life—from magazine articles, newspaper clippings, and, most often, her own observations—filled her lectures.

"Now you see how it works," she'd say. "That's how it is when you're attuned to God." "Don't you want to live your life from this perspective?" she'd ask, her face framing the wonder and happiness that come from such an awakening.

Because she spoke as she lived, her audiences listened intently, not doubting the priority she gave to character. What they cherished, however, like children who never have visited a foreign country, was to be taken on a journey through the eyes of her clairvoyance, anywhere and everywhere—past, present, and future.

The question and answer periods each conclave session threw open a floodgate of inquiry: Please describe for us what a Guardian Angel really looks like. Are the folk tales of fairies and elves accurate descriptions of nature beings? Can you tell us more about our auras and how they reveal our physical, emotional, and mental states? Who was Hitler in his past life? What is the inner cause of migraine headaches? How should I pray for a friend who is dying of cancer? Is it true that you can see our thoughts and observe when people are not telling you the truth? What is the karmic reason behind my marriage to a man who says he no longer loves me and wants a divorce? Was there really once a continent of Atlantis and will it rise again? Is there life on other planets? What is meant by 'the second coming of Christ?' What about flying saucers—are they real? I had this dream....

On and on they went, sometimes keyed to her lesson's topic but more often a burning question that wouldn't wait or the response to the irresistible stimulation of her willingness to share this rare, forthright gift so freely if the student was sincere.

From occasional skeptics or antagonists came pointed questions intended to trap her in a dilemma or cut her down to their size. These she answered with an arsenal of wisdom and fearlessness. One such instance called her to task over reincarnation, claiming it to be a false Eastern teaching altogether alien to Christianity and certainly never taught by Jesus of Nazareth.

She paused after reading this question, then acknowledged its superficial logic as a common misconception. She marked as untrue the absence of any evidence that reincarnation is a Christian teaching, citing a passage from the eleventh chapter of Matthew in which the Lord Christ proclaims John the Baptist to have been unexcelled among men, concluding his praise with the words: "for all the prophets and the law prophesied until John. And if ye will receive it, this is Elias, which was for to come. He that hath ears to hear, let him hear."

Her face then blazed with the certainty of what her own eyes had seen: "But the reason I know whereof I speak" she continued, "lies in my memory of having lived in his time and to have known him personally. Our Lord did not mention reincarnation often to the masses, though many realized his knowledge of it. What teachings he gave them along those lines were expunged from the record by the infamous Council of Nicaea in the fourth century, A.D., in an attempt to more tightly control the minds of the masses. It was, nevertheless, one of the mystery teachings and it was in his ministry to the Band of Seventy that most was given on this subject."

She then relaxed and lifted up her face with a little musical laugh, saying, "Besides, I have the clear memory of many of my own past incarnations and that convinces me of its truth—wouldn't it you!" And the hush that had fallen over the audience at this challenge was broken with the hearty sound of laughter.

Chapter 9

Trial by Fire

Summer passed into fall and the services in the Oak Grove Sanctuary were moved to a rented clubhouse in Vista, should the rainy season arrive ahead of schedule. Even though the hills were dry and thirsting for the relief of an early rain, the custom of evening walks at Quest Haven lost none of its refreshment. About an hour before sundown, after one of Flower's delicious dinners possibly of pot roast, German potatoes, a wilted lettuce salad, and finished with fresh peach cobbler, she and Lawrence loved to gather their dogs and cats: Lucky, a handsome dalmatian, Curly, a black cocker spaniel, and Raja Leo, a regal tangerine-colored cat who was once Flower's pet as a lion in Egypt. Down the entrance road they would go, the dogs out in front, tails wagging, and the wise old cat following behind for a commanding view of everyone.

Unconcerned rabbits stood near the thickets of chaparral, nibbling shoots of grass until one of the dogs gave chase. Then they'd dart to the safety of cover. Quail always were out in number, some crossing the road to disappear silently into the tall grass, others flushed by the bounding dogs with entire coveys taking to the air in a whir of beating wings, then gliding soundlessly to some secret sanctuary.

Flower would call Lawrence's attention to one thing of beauty after another—some without and others within, and he, likewise. Often they walked quietly down the road and off on one of the trails, drawing upon the power of the evening's peace.

The inner side of these experiences was rich beyond her

desire or capacity to express it. If one were among the blind, wouldn't it be unthinkable to attempt a running commentary of the inexhaustible detail and array of phenomena making up the visual world? She faced, on a higher dimension, exactly this situation and met it with uncommonly good sense: when something special appeared, that she shared, frequently with delight or awe—perhaps a glimpse of the resplendent Archangel overshadowing Quest Haven or a Deva King passing along the tops of the hills, or even the sight of a little gnome named Happy whose curiosity about people and fondness for Flower was bottomless.

Lawrence working in the print shop

Soon after America's entrance into World War II, Lawrence had taken a job as a fireman at Camp Pendleton, a large marine base several miles to the north. He chose this work because of its 24-hour duty cycle every other day, a schedule giving him the needed time to continue his other activities at Quest Haven: printing, maintaining the retreat, and assisting Flower whose commitments multiplied with the months. She spent alternate days and nights alone, no other person within miles, without telephone or even the reassurance of electricity if she heard a strange noise or had an unexpected caller, often a lost motorist. Not once did this strike her as unusual or ill-advised. She knew she and her mission were safe, that God would protect both. This given, there remained the changeless tranquility of the surrounding hills and the precious gift of uninterrupted hours to speed her work.

Then came a never-to-be-forgotten Sunday early in November of 1943. They had driven to Long Beach for a lecture engagement. On their way home that evening, off in the direction of Quest Haven, they saw an appalling spectacle in the sky: the orange-red glow of fire beneath an overhanging blackness of smoke that blurred the entire horizon. The wartime speed limit of 35 miles-per-hour gave them time for prayer but robbed them of at least an hour before reaching the scene of action.

Pulling into Quest Haven, Lawrence quickly assessed their situation from those already on the scene who had come to help save the retreat. Already several expensive homes in the Rancho Santa Fe area a few miles south had been destroyed. The fire, driven by gusty winds, was out of control, advancing swiftly toward them across the tinder-dry hills.

Flower instantly gathered together the women and began a cordon of prayer—all together at first, then each taking hour-long turns through the night ahead in an unbroken appeal for the Weather Angels to intercede. Lawrence, an expert fireman himself, took charge of the men, directing them to strategic positions to cut fire breaks and clear the ground of leaves and dry grass. It was urgent, exhausting work.

As the flames drew closer, rising in spectacular waves that engulfed entire hillsides in one great roar, the women desperately prayed. Tears streaming down her face, Flower called out now to the Wind Angels to turn back the holocaust before it reduced this hallowed estate to ashes. And as she spoke the winds fell calm around them. The tide of approaching flames lost its momentum for the rest of the night. Now tears of gratitude filled the women's eyes as they huddled about Flower on the porch of Blue Gables. Hope leaped up, too, that the crisis might somehow have passed.

Lawrence seized the opportunity to make contact with the Forest Service crews scattered along the fire front in an attempt to marshal reinforcements for the handful of Quest Haven men working without rest through the dark hours of the early morning. At first he had no success. Because of wartime curtailments, the fire line was seriously undermanned and equipment was in short supply. Later, it was learned that a total of 38 fires sprang up throughout Southern California on this same Sunday, following a pattern of arson and exhausting all reserve manpower.

By the next day, the fire again was gaining ground and Lawrence persuaded about a hundred marines and civilian volunteer fire fighters to make a stand at the Quest Haven boundary. His strength surpassed understanding as he organized men and equipment to cut additional fire breaks and isolate the hottest fire centers now moving into their canyon. In spite of his gallantry and leadership, an incredible situation developed. With the men now available on the line there was more than a good chance Quest Haven could be spared. Word had come to Flower through her Guardian that this, in fact, was so.

At this turning point, victory in sight, Lawrence was stunned to see a number of men dousing gasoline into their oak grove, intent upon setting a backfire. Joined by Flower they pleaded with the headstrong, self-appointed "fire wardens" who had taken this ill-advised action impulsively. From his fire training, Lawrence knew the conditions were adverse for a backfire. Flower, from her Guardian, knew it to be in defiance of this one's instructions. But what could they do? Obstinately bent on their plan, they set fire to the gasoline-soaked underbrush; perplexed, they looked on as it sputtered and eventually died out—the growth underneath the irreplaceable trees was too green to catch fire. For an instant she thought this would be a sign to them of the foolhardy nature of their plan; but they moved the men to the far side of the trees and stubbornly put torches to the dense chaparral.

110

Heartbroken with grief, Flower returned to the house, to watch the new flames spread, rage out of control, then turn back on the very land supposedly to be spared. The witless backfire now fell upon Quest Haven as its destroyer. A heroic stand by Lawrence and a friend barely saved the oak grove from becoming a charred ruin in the wake of the mounting fire storm. For the weary, embattled, courageous Quest Haven family, this was the darkest hour. Most of the retreat was either burning or directly in the path of closing walls of fire. There was little left to do but rise above their aching fatigue and pray.

Through that day and another night the fire flared back and forth, somehow never landing its death blow. By the next morning the final and most perilous front was to the north as the winds, shifting suddenly, began moving the fire down on top of them. Lawrence was leading a small band of men equipped only with portable hand pumps toward the beleaguered northern boundary for one last effort to stay the total destruction of what remained. The prayer cordon at Blue Gables had now passed its thirty-sixth hour. Slowly, amazingly, the great fire came to a halt, its fury spent, and within the hour died out entirely.

Returning to Flower, their home, and their valiant friends, he led the happy, exhausted company in the one prayer left within them: thanksgiving to God! Quest Haven, though cruelly scarred, had been spared its oak grove, its buildings, and at least half of its chaparral-covered hills.

❧ ✳ ☙

During the meeting with The Lord Christ on Mt. Frazier at the onset of her twenty-first year, Flower was given a two-fold ministry: to enlighten humanity about the Angel Kingdom and help individuals toward higher unfoldment.

In the early years she quite naturally devoted her teaching to the first of these commissions. It was closest to her heart, flowed easiest through the channel of her clairvoyance, and audiences had an unquenchable thirst for revelations of these wondrous Beings whose significance exceeded all previous knowing. In 1937, she was inspired to write a book about this Kingdom, calling it *Natives of Eternity*, a title recognizing their ethereal and deathless permanence in Creation.

Without ever slighting the charge to uphold the Angels before the eyes of her audiences, she continued to shift the emphasis toward the unfoldment of discipleship. Turning more and more to individuals and their problems in drawing closer to God, she frequently went to the Akashic Records for answers. This unveiled a personal relevance to inner sight that fascinated those seeking her help. At first, these usually were informal conversations that took place at one of the week-long conclaves or pilgrimages. Flower sat in a lawn chair while those in attendance joined her, one at a time. Most often the questions were open-ended, asking about past lives or spiritual needs, the latter holding greater promise for the maturity of the seeker. First, she would examine the person's aura minutely, then close her eyes for a moment to receive instruction from their Guardian or to gather information from the Akashic Records.

Questions about previous lifetimes, if asked only out of curiosity or vanity, seldom uncovered historical celebrities such as pharaohs or saints or generals or philosophers. As she reminded her listeners before inviting these sessions, "We always find ourselves less developed in the past than we are today and shouldn't be surprised to learn that even in our most recent incarnations we probably led very common, uneventful lives." To push much beyond one's more recent appearances was to follow disappointment with despair, even repulsion.

"The past for most of us," she observed, "is neither very pretty nor flattering. To look back only is constructive when it teaches us how to meet something in the present that has us puzzled or hemmed in."

To questions prompted by these latter motives came marvelous, illuminating answers clearly pinpointing the sources of existing entanglements, testings, or weaknesses. Conflicts between individuals traced to rival or neglected relationships in the past, creating the karmic necessity to come together in another incarnation as members of a family, as business competitors, or fellow employees. A mother of a stillborn child learned that this soul previously had taken his own life and now must repeat the arduous process of preparing, all over again, to enter life in less inviting circumstances. A woman fanatically intolerant of a drunken husband found out she had been an alcoholic herself recently and now had both to suffer this humiliation and learn to forgive another person at the same crossroads. Her repressed memory for the bitterness of this struggle was hidden in the self-righteous resentment she projected on him. The family of a young man struggling with symptoms of schizophrenia discovered that this youth, at the same age in his last life, had become intrigued with a spiritualistic movement solely given to adventures in phenomena. Once again, he faced the dark encounter of losing his will to forces beyond his control—to voices and specters that flooded his senses with bizarre and chaotic inundations—and the outcome was still uncertain.

There were pleasant findings, too. A man's deep appreciation for Roman history was linked to his life as an officer in one of Julius Caesar's legions. His great admiration for General Douglas MacArthur was true to this heritage, since this was the celebrated Roman commander returned. A teenager who had been an endless trial to her parents because of her flighty ways, unconventional tastes, and passion for the out-of-doors, Flower immediately recognized to be a young soul recently in from the deva line of evolution, unexpectedly drawn into human life because of her great curiosity about people. This accounting finally put her mother and father at ease as it neatly explained all of her eccentricities and allowed them to accept her for what she was.

More and more as Flower tuned in to ways to help persons progress Godward, she encompassed topics in her spoken and written lessons ranging across metaphysics, psychology, and character unfoldment. Drawing primarily from her past training for the framework, but infusing this structure with insights and examples from all available sources, she synthesized a way of discipleship distinctive in its well-roundedness, practicality, and integrity to the Christ archetype.

In the psychology of Carl Jung she recognized a rich source of material that later led to a close friendship with Dr. Fritz Kunkel and his wife, of Los Angeles. Kunkel was a Jungian analyst who had written extensively on the very problems she found confronting truth students—their personality selves. In psychology, she saw a key to the single, most formidable obstacle to enlightenment: the human ego and all of its encumbrances down to the shadow nature itself. In her increasing focus on individual growth, here was welcome help.

By now, winter rains had rinsed away the thickest ashes of the fire and with spring a surprising display of fresh sprouts and wild flowers, many never before seen, revitalized the barren landscape. When the Director of the Santa Barbara Botanical Gardens, adjacent to the site of their conclaves in that city, visited Quest Haven to help plan for its replanting, he told them an interesting fact: there are certain flowers with seeds so tough they only germinate after a fire cracks them open with its searing heat. What they were witnessing was indeed a rare floral display. He also was encouraging about the effects of the fire's destruction. Because most of the oak trees had been spared, the chaparral would soon regrow and they would also see more deer in the area with the abundance of young, tender shoots to feed upon.

Most of the six hundred and more trees Flower and Lawrence had planted were lost and with them the years of digging basins and carrying heavy buckets of water. Now they must begin again.

Their botanical friend advised them to capitalize on the flora native to the area. He described this characteristic growth as the "elfin forest," a name describing a number of dwarf trees and shrubs mingled together to form a particular variety of chaparral: toyon berry, white and blue wild lilac, manzanita, sumac, lemonade berry, elderberry, mountain mahogany, scrub oak and many more. This combination was found in only three locations in southern California, he said, and the specimens at their retreat were among the finest he'd ever seen.

The name delighted Flower, exactly matching the outer beauty with its inner aspect—a playground for myriads of elfin beings. On the spot, they decided the hills and valley nestling Quest Haven would be called Elfin Forest Canyon.

Her vision of the central area of the Retreat departed from their guest's preference for native vegetation in one important respect: there must be a forest-like profusion of trees with large sheltering branches; evergreens should predominate since their higher evolution appealed to the devas and Angelic presences in charge of nature.

She did not press this point with their knowledgeable visitor. It was an insight from her own devic background and nourished by an inner sensitivity to such things, a contribution beyond the conventional appreciation of a botanist, but one underscoring her unswerving loyalty to the values of the inner side of life.

Still, of all the trees on the grounds, the native California live oaks grew in greatest number, spreading their huge rambling branches in broad canopies fashioned from myriads of minute, olive-green leaves that shimmered in the sunlight. Underneath, cool caves of shade refreshed by soft afternoon winds from the Pacific offered all the comforts of air conditioned living, and the scenery of a fairyland, besides.

Beneath one of the largest of these glorious oaks, at the edge of a small clearing where a cluster of beehives once stood, Flower had her study—a tiny white building about four feet wide and six feet long with a screened door for ventilation and protection from seasonal insects. In an ordinary chair before a simple table she answered letters, wrote articles, planned her lessons, and meditated. Lawrence affectionately called it her "power house," in recognition of all she accomplished within its walls.

Though they often were apart while carrying out their separate responsibilities at the Retreat, they made up for this necessity in an ingenious way-by leaving love notes in secret places for the other to come upon unexpectedly and by sending little messages back and forth whenever an opportunity arose.

One day, their secretary was delivering the day's mail to Flower's study when Lawrence stopped her long enough to write on an office memo what appeared to be a book title, "Isle of View," asking that she hand Flower this item first. When she returned from delivering the mail, she had an identical note written on the reverse side of the same memo, this time by Flower.

"I don't understand what's going on here," commented the secretary. "I know it's none of my business but what on earth are you saying to each other?"

Lawrence's eyes danced with amusement. "Try saying these words quickly and you'll see."

The curious woman repeated them rapidly twice, then

as the cryptic message gave itself away she laughed at her own puzzlement. How two people must love each other, she thought, to find such engaging ways to feed the flame of their togetherness.

As their work grew, more persons attended the weekly services, many seeking out Flower for advice and help with their individual problems. Quest Haven, for all of its quietness and beauty, was her working environment and her sensitivity to the pull of mounting correspondence, personal interviews, lesson preparation, and housekeeping duties aroused the need for renewal only the high, pine-covered mountains offered. Tragically, Mt. Frazier and the grove she treasured above any other memory in her life for what happened underneath its sheltering branches, had been devastated by the worst fire in the mountain's history. She had no desire to see its charred remains.

Then an interesting thing happened. She had scheduled a Sunday afternoon lecture in Palm Springs, the desert resort community at the foot of the San Jacinto Mountain range, which rises to a height of nearly 11,000 feet. Coming back the next morning on the Palms-to-Pines highway with Lawrence's parents, Lawrence turned to Flower and said, "How about running up and seeing Idyllwild? I hear it's a lovely mountain resort."

She was tired from the trip which had ended in a number of interviews, but seeing how much it meant to him, she agreed. From the turnoff at the main highway, it was six miles up a winding road, then over the ridge of a mile-high valley. Flower caught her breath in surprise. It was the most unexpectedly beautiful setting she had ever seen. The valley was ringed by lofty peaks, forming a natural bowl. Everywhere, stands of pine, fir, and cedar soared skyward in a fresh, fragrant sea of green treetops. Her body's weariness vanished. This was a chosen place, hidden as a gift for this moment; and

117

to think that they might have passed by it but for Lawrence's intuitive leading. She glanced at her Guardian to catch the knowing smile of one who, wishing to please another in a special way, has kept a secret to the last.

Idyllwild itself was a small cluster of shops, cabins, and an inn, all welcoming them with friendly, rustic charm. At a realtor's office they inquired about property and made arrangements to rent a quaint little cabin as their personal mountain retreat.

How Flower rejoiced over this day! It was more than the personal uplift of finding again her inner temples, her Courts of Renewal and Empowerment, it was the promise of things yet to come because of this finding. Another door was opening. She sensed it in her Guardian's outshining joy, in the frequencies radiating through the atmosphere of this power center, in the awareness of mighty nature presences all about. There weren't enough ways to give thanks for the upsweep of gratitude this brought. She was looking into the future again, seeing that all would be well, having only to keep true to the Cause.

Chapter 10

Living the Life

Questhaven, as its name came to be written during the war now over, was much more than Flower and Lawrence's home and their work's headquarters; even more than a retreat where one experienced God in nature. It was a training center—a school rekindling the mystery teachings given her in Greece and Palestine.

The difference, reflecting the gathering dawn light of the Aquarian Age, was its openness. Unlike the instruction given by Pythagoras to his chosen pupils and the Christ to the Seventy, Flower had the charge to reveal these hidden truths to whoever indicated a sincere and trustworthy attitude, oftentimes to entire audiences, some of whom came for the first time out of curiosity. The mystery now was not in concealing information from all but the elect; it was in the uncertainty of the human factor. Who stood at the gate of interior readiness? Who would recognize her authority, the validity of her words, and then be inspired to begin living in this new, illumined way?

The reaction to what she shared of esoteric truth left no doubt of the rising interest in this subject. People listened intently, many leaning forward in their chairs, shifting their heads first one way, then another, to hear more clearly, to gain a better view.

Her face shone in an unearthly beauty excelling the fineness of her features, lovely in themselves. The inner light from her amber-flecked eyes touched every person present, quickening with each joyous smile and returning, gaze for gaze, all and more than she received.

Many came back week after week to the Oak Grove Sanctuary in the summer months and to the rented chapel or clubhouse in Vista in the other seasons, eagerly listening and learning, taking in her every glance and gesture. She was like no other person they'd ever laid eyes on; she spoke of powers and realities and destinies that were sweeping revelations and she spoke of them in detail with astonishing intimacy. She knew these things through a oneness with them; they were as much a part of her as seeing and breathing. This was her mystery and her reality, a citizen of Eternity, yet a citizen of time and space, giving the treasures of one world to the other.

Now began a process between teacher and pupil, unknown in its depths and heights to the latter, that followed the ancient, ageless path up the Mountain of God—what she called the *Christward Way* or the way within to Christ. First came an interest to draw closer to Flower and Lawrence; to become a part of their work and the Retreat's growth. There was never a formal pledge or a congregation to join officially; Questhaven had no membership. People came as they felt led and left when they chose. The only condition asked was their sincere, respectful appreciation of the Work's purpose. If they wished also to support it with their attendance, tithes, and other contributions, that was reason for rejoicing.

What placed the newcomer on the upward path of Flower's studied attention was an inspired awareness of dedication he or she, sooner or later, shared with her, making a heartfelt commitment to the goal ahead. This signaled the individual's awareness of a soulic impression, lucid in its sense of direction, impelling the act of consecration.

Such a moment flooded the pupil with the magnificent feeling of a great journey begun and no matter how the journey went, another pilgrim was awake to its movement and saw the light over the gate leading toward the Celestial City.

120

Flower prized these beginnings. She was vividly aware of the obstacles yet to overcome—few knew them better—but starting out was the thing; getting underway after years, even lives of marking time; at long last awake to who they were, where they were going, and why.

What came next varied with each individual. No set format was apparent outwardly, yet there was an inner standard always guiding her work with the awakening pupil. She looked upon the task of the wayshower as an intuitive art, ever to be freshened with new vocabulary, new perspectives, and new models. Nothing was allowed to stagnate or crystallize. Life, she never tired of demonstrating, was renewal. Once a person ceased to grow, to discover untapped riches, to explore uncrossed horizons, then had senescence begun, regardless of an individual's age by the calendar. She dared those following the Way to overcome their timidity or rigidity toward change.

"I know you've never been drawn to house pets but this little kitten so needs a home. If you could make room for her in your life what a blessing it would be to her evolution." "Here are my tickets to the symphony next week, when I'll be traveling. Won't you use them?" "There is the most exceptional artist at the new gallery in Idyllwild. You owe it to yourself

Flower performing an animal blessing

to see his paintings of the mountains." "This woman makes the most gorgeous bouquets, all with flowers right out of her own garden, and she would gladly take the time to show you her secret."

If invitations and coaxing didn't get through to the pupil, and they seemed to be bogged down with old habits preventing the needed change, Flower would startle them out of their inertia with declarations striking like lightning bolts. To a man loyal to most rules of the Way but still clinging to his appetite for cigarettes, she said: "John, how can you expect your friends to want to share the same room with a smokestack!" A young woman who complained of no suitable marriage prospects heard her say, "But Natalie, the kind of man you claim to want would never be drawn to anyone as spoiled and hypercritical as you! And don't you see how much happier you'll be once you've thrown off this shell of self-centeredness and start being a person who is fun to be around?"

After the sparks of her forthright appraisal cooled, the person who had sought her help learned two things: the truth about himself and the value of frankness as an impetus to growth.

One quality Flower hunted for and nourished constantly was teachableness: the willingness, when finding a trusted teacher, to be taught—to accept assignments, carry out directions, receive evaluation, and on one's own, observe and study the wayshower, searching by contrast for the gaps in their own character and channelship. If the newcomer feared

122

the loss of identity in this process, typically the more independent, self-willed individuals, they simply came so far, but no farther, remaining on the outside or eventually gravitating toward another teaching where ego-enhancement was practiced. Others, troubled with a too pliable nature, were slavishly dependent on Flower for even trivial advice.

Souls with top-heavy egos she handled cautiously, giving them duties or opportunities that could be evaluated readily and terminated when necessary, but never the positions of leadership and trust they desired until the vital step of self-giving was reached. Those leaning on her too much she patiently steered into activities requiring greater self-reliance. Between these two extremes were many forming the backbone of her following, the strong central column supporting the gathering numbers of people drawn to Sunday services, midweek classes, and the annual retreats and tours.

Flower lived as she taught, an attainment that overshadowed everything else about her. It was this likeness to the Christ that caught people by surprise, particularly if they were attracted originally by her gifts of clairvoyance and revelation. At first, the fascination aroused by these superphysical powers obscured the more relevant achievement undergirding them: her self-mastery. When she described discipleship she spoke not of ideals gleaned from the renowned teachers and philosophers of the world; she spoke of things known to her in the brilliant reality of her earthly experience—this was her authority. Neither did she depend solely on the lives of great men and women to illustrate what God had in mind for each of His sons and daughters, once they were steadfast. Every trait, every attitude, every quality, every discipline-defining character as the Christ manifested it, she knew through her own relentless enterprise. And, though she never claimed the work to be finished, each of these facets to the jewel within her gleamed with such purity, those who had eyes to see her

123

character proceeded to grind and polish away at their own interior jewel with new incentive, already reflecting glints of the diamond's fire first seen in Flower's outshining radiance.

The truest of disciples was Lawrence himself. He never strained or evidenced the battle within; to outward appearance the process of growth was an effortless soaring on the wings of spirit, riding the updrafts ever higher. When people asked him how he managed never to appear weary at the end of an 18 hour day, or discouraged following an obvious reversal, and how he always was cheerful, ready to give time to the procession of interruptions and demands coming his way, with his eyes shining in merriment, he might answer, "I just keep picking one foot up and putting it down in front of the other." After his little joke, making light the heaviest of burdens had another man carried them, he got to the point, smiling as he spoke: "When you live 24 hours a day with an Angel you have nothing but happiness to think about."

Because the question came from one who knew them both, the answer sufficed. Unspoken, there remained a mystery to Lawrence's ease and constancy as Flower's companion and pupil. The psychology of the ascent up the Mountain of God is fraught with pitfalls, oppositions, doubts, and dark trials. How was he able to shield himself from these hazards? What kind of a man, without moments of visible mutiny or defeat, can set aside his ego, place his needs second to those of his wife, and give his energy, his heart, and his will to tireless, unhesitating service of the Cause first glimpsed through the other's eyes?

Lawrence, during rare moments of introspection, acknowledged the battle waged against his lower nature. But as he spoke of these things, he never became downcast with guilt; instead, he smiled over his shortcomings just as a parent smiles knowingly over a child's foolishness. He had reached the point in his own individuation where he could be detached from imperfectness, without, at the same time, becoming indifferent. In character, he was not far behind his sweetheart and wayshower.

The extraordinary feat Lawrence achieved in his unbroken relationship with both Flower and the holy quest they pursued hourly, was the transmutation of his shadow: that dweller in the instinctive roots of the body's animal ancestry; the primeval adversary, author of deflection and inertia, rebellion and neglect; the slayer of good intentions and holy desires; the eye that sees evil everywhere but within itself, and is, therefore, the personal seed of Satan. In each of Lawrence's dedications, he had to surrender all personal attachments, declaring total war against his shadow nature. No one was ever to know the shape of the battles that ensued, only their outcome: triumph signaled by his victorious eyes and shining face, year after year.

Lawrence had tapped the alchemical mystery of spirit, lifting him beyond the extremes of ego and shadow fomenting the stormy conflicts within the earth-bound pilgrim. Instead of dissipating his energies between success and failure, first approaching, then avoiding growth, he moved through the hours with the same serenity and poise he first wonderingly observed in his beloved. Lawrence, in becoming what she had attained, was Flower's finest demonstration to others of the workings and results of discipleship—how, if the sculptor is steadfast, the figure emerges.

The art of this mystery was channelship: the very heartbeat of Flower's giftedness, the means of her access to the inner worlds, the foundation of her spiritual integrity, and the source of her renewal. It was clearly the master key allowing Lawrence to open the gates of Divinity within himself, while safely unlocking the doors to his subterranean nature that the down-streaming light would scatter its darkness. It was the discipline without which there is nothing, but with it, all things become possible. Every one of Flower's instructions to her pupils aimed at this goal: to become a pure instrument of Divine Intelligence systematically rooting out every entrenched motive conspiring to plunder this treasure for itself.

It began for Lawrence, in earnest, with their married life together. The days of their courtship and the need to be separated in the early months of marriage, lengthened the time when two people ordinarily see each other at their best, keeping alive what for many is a wishful illusion that eventually must be reconciled with the more human side of their temperaments.

What happened to Lawrence instead was at first incredible: his wife hadn't been living on her tiptoes just for him—she lived in this glorious consciousness unbrokenly. He never found her down from its heights, empty of inspiration and seeking some form of distraction to fill the void. Her housekeeping, shopping, conversations with casual acquaintances, enjoyment of a movie or a magazine article—all these commonplace activities she experienced with enlightened purposefulness.

One of two things had to happen: unable to keep pace, her husband would be caught up in a mounting feeling of inadequacy and frustration, stubbornly obstructing her through withdrawal or rebellion; or, learning her secret, he would ascend along the same path at her side. Because of what Lawrence brought to their marriage from his own past, it was the latter.

He became her round-the-clock apprentice, alertly assimilating the habits and practices observed in his wife. Every morning began, upon awakening, with the realization of the inner worlds and the encircling beauty they wrapped about her senses. As consciousness accelerated, she reviewed her life rules—those innermost vows made to the God Presence keeping this day true to her life's mission. As she dressed and prepared for the day she mentally formed a plan for its hours that opened up the currents of intuition bathing the atmosphere about her thoughts.

She now was ready for the principal meditation of the day, about thirty minutes in length, during which her consciousness was intently centered on the task of active, total alignment, followed by the painstaking enfoldment in God Light of all things precious to her.

She began by reverently invoking the Holy Trinity, an experience showering her with luminescent symbols from these three Presences and that touched Lawrence as impressions of quickening. She next introduced him to a meditation technique shown to her by a Higher One. It was to prayerfully call upon each plane of her being, joining lower to higher, until all levels were united harmoniously.

With Lawrence attentively at her side following each step she closed her eyes, her right hand open and upturned in her lap as a chalice of inflow; her left palm open and turned downward to release the stream of energy. She described to him, clairvoyantly, how the Light indeed entered and left the body in exactly this manner during meditation or prayer and how every recognition of these inner processes by the pupil's outer posture and expression enhanced their effectiveness.

Then she spoke the words of the alignment:

"My physical body with its invisible sheath of vitality, is the servant of Lord God Indwelling." She paused for a moment, commenting, "Notice how the body now seems lighter, more relaxed and porous. Its aura, if you could see it, is already brightened by this baptism."

She continued, "My outer body and its etheric envelope is attuned to the astral body which is the disciple of Lord God Indwelling." There was another pause, then she said, "This body contains all that we call our emotions. Its great needs are poise, serenity, and obedience; freedom from the extremes of moods, passions, and craving for excitement. Already, like true disciples, they have become visibly stilled.

"My astral body is attuned to the mental body which is the pupil of Lord God Indwelling." Again she waited for Lawrence to feel its full effect. "It is always needful," she observed, "to clear the mind of its restless preoccupation with distracting thoughts. Feel the mind swept clean by the winds of spirit until there is only the awareness of reverence and wonder for the Holy of Holies within you."

"My mind is attuned to my causal body, the soul, which is my Angel Self." There was a still longer pause, then she spoke, reluctant to break the silence following this pronouncement. "This is the highest level we ordinarily contact. It is enough to gather in whatever impressions we can of our soul's unresting wish for us to know oneness with its consciousness. Its qualities," she added, "are beauty, holiness, and purity of a degree impossible to describe. Once you've beheld its reality, you'll never know self-satisfaction again."

Then came the final linking up with Divinity: "Through my soul being, I am aligned with the Adonai, or I-am-of-God Self. My Adonai is at one with the God Flame within, or Holy God Indwelling."

In the silence that followed, Lawrence strained to feel some impression of this ultimate aspect of himself. Flower, sensing his struggle, spoke again. "These are planes which we enter consciously only on two occasions: during a major initiation and when we are Masters. We know of them now only to have the perspective of their reality and to realize the immensity of the way ahead."

Her eyes still closed, Flower entered the second phase of this meditation, enfolding the world's need for enlightenment and brotherhood in the mantling of the Christ Spirit and, step by step, taking each enterprise and person needing renewal or overshadowing into the temple of Divinity's attention.

Finally, she invited Lawrence to join her in visualizing the unfoldment of their work, the opening of the way for their forthcoming lecture tour, the increase in supply to widen their scope of service, and, here and now, the harmonious, productive, Christ-illumined experience of this day.

As the meditation ended, Lawrence looked about the room. Wherever his eyes glanced, lay a vibrant glow of light he'd never noticed before. He blinked his eyes several times but still the soft sheen clung to the carpet, the curtains, the furniture, the lampshades—everything. A deep sense of wonder bloomed within him to realize this existence of light everywhere.

And the day at hand, how it beckoned him to enter into its hours. He knew on this morning he had touched truth closer to its center than ever before. He knew that what he'd been shown was the crossing of a threshold bridging the outer with the inner, the start of impressions and receptions causing him to feel reborn, to want to reexperience life anew, recovering the splendor he had earlier missed.

Coming full swing into the realization of how life perceived inwardly is the means of one's renewal and transformation gave Lawrence the momentum he needed to keep pace with his bright companion and carry through as her partner in their service of the Christ. It also helped him understand her own responsiveness to inner guidance. Throughout their life together, he cherished the moments when she would come into the room and announce, "Lawrence, I have a message from the Master." Sitting down in a chair, he would laugh in his great-hearted way, saying, "Here we go again!" It could be an unforeseen lecture tour, a new publication, or even a trip of spiritual exploration to South America, as happened in the fall of 1947.

Of all such messages, that one seemed most fantastic since the expenses exceeded $1800 per person and, unlike the lecture tours which paid for themselves, there would be no income. Without savings behind them, but with the same faith that once brought her family west, Flower began packing suitcases with the various articles such a journey required. They went ahead with passports and inoculations, even encouraging the same steps for two friends who wished to make the trip with them; only then did the way open. Just three weeks ahead of their scheduled departure a woman benefactor informed them she would pay their full expenses.

Sensitivity to the inner aspect of life returned many practical bonuses. Locating comfortable hotels and good restaurants was a most unusual adventure when touring. Driving up in front of a prospective hotel, she would examine its inner color and emanations, okaying or passing it by on these merits. Restaurants, too, stood revealed for better or worse by their frequencies of light energy. Early in their travels together Lawrence had asked, "How do you tell the good restaurants from the ordinary ones?"

From his clear-seeing wife came the answer, "I see the aura of gourmet tea rooms, or coffee shops, as a lavender mist. Mediocre places have a brownish emanation mixed with a dark shade of orange."

Shopping, one of their favorite recreations, was a similar adventure in extrasensory discrimination. Together they strolled past the windows in a shopping center, or among the market places of Latin America on their trip, alert for impressions that invited closer investigation. The bright green aura of a particular store was a trustworthy reflection of the merchant's quality of taste and the fairness of his prices. The result was a substantial saving of time, getting them promptly into the shops having the most to offer. Articles or objects of special significance had about them a stronger light, a phenomenon most often investing the work of a spiritually awakened artisan or craftsman. Paintings, sculpture, handwoven fabrics, and ceramics frequently bore this distinguishing feature.

And books, whether in bookstores or libraries, nearly reached off their shelves into her arms, so visibly translucent were their jackets to the presence of inner light channeled by the author. The nature of her work required her to uncover fresh sources of material week after week, keeping her lectures and writing vital and current; of all the applications of her extended vision, this one salvaged the greatest number of hours. And just as it speeded her search for the key paragraphs in preparing her homework as a school girl, it now served her to sift out the prime illustrations and light revealing statements.

What a difference it made to be alive to the inner side of reality, to be a channel of its riches. If there was one wish Flower longed with her whole being to come true, it was through the sharing of her own findings and the way that led her to them, that others might succeed at this quest, too. One soul whose life was set afire by crossing this threshold, in that moment, became worth the whole effort, making up for all the half-hearted ones who abandoned the search just when the most stood to be gained.

Lift your gaze to the stars because there is so much above you to go towards. Do not stand in your tracks too long — move upward.

Chapter 11

The Coming of the Masters

By the summer of 1950, Questhaven had taken a long stride into its future. Electricity, first by a gasoline-driven generator and finally along power lines, ended the era of kerosene and gas lamps. This made possible a print shop with its own press and linotype. A 165,000 gallon reservoir fed by an electrically operated pump now provided ample water for the Retreat's many gardens and trees, multiplying each year. But the most welcome among the improvements was a large adobe block addition to the recently built El Deseo guest cottage and the connecting print shop, forming Questhaven's new office and chapel with seating capacity for over one hundred people. Six days during the week it echoed the sounds of typewriters and voices at work, moving along with the flow of correspondence, publication orders and the daily routine of retreat management. On the seventh day issued the sound of choir voices and the congregation singing, the

New chapel, office and print shop

133

reverberations joyfully escaping through the chapel windows and fading into the surrounding hills. Next came Lawrence's voice followed by Flower's, and Sunday at Questhaven was no longer a seasonal visit, but a year-round celebration of God in nature; of God in the midst of men, women, and children worshiping together.

The annual Pilgrimage in its pine sanctuary at Idyllwild that summer was an outstanding success, both in its large attendance and the brilliance of Flower's message. She spoke on the "Immensity Consciousness," a state of awareness she had been inspired to investigate recently that led her into new approaches of instructing students in the art of meditation. Letters flocked in, testifying to the impact these teachings already were having.

That August, Questhaven quietly observed its tenth anniversary with thanksgiving for all that had been accomplished and a growing expectancy of things to come.

About the middle of the month a picture, thought to be a portrait of the Christ, arrived in the mail. It was a small photographic replica of an original and much larger drawing by an artist named Arthur Learned of Stamford, Connecticut: its face kept appearing before him until at last he drew its likeness. It had been sent to Flower for her comments.

As she examined the photograph she said to Lawrence, "This is an authentic picture of a Master who seems so familiar to me, but right now I seem unable to remember his name, though I know it will come to me."

The next morning, the fifteenth of August, the picture was placed on the chapel altar at Flower's request, in time for the regular eight o'clock meditation. Suddenly Flower became conscious of a strong, sunshine-like beam warmly penetrating through the middle of her being. It was round with a light of purest white sprinkled with silver flecks. She glanced about to discover it encompassed the two people sitting nearest her.

Concentrating on this living shaft, she began receiving impressions from its center. "This beam is from a Master who had been Joshua in an earlier incarnation and also Ezra or Esdras," she said. "This Master works under the Lord Maha Chohan who is the officiant of the Third Aspect of the Trinity. He can be reached only from the soul level when one is very quiet and meditating from the depth of his inner self. He has come to teach us inner peace, directed attention, and also of other Infinities."

Flower then explained that he was the Master responsible for the instruction in Idyllwild and for the lessons on Immensity Consciousness; Lawrence remembered her mentioning during these classes that she was to contact a new Master whom at that time, she could see far in the distance as if in miniature form. And her Guardian had added, "This Master is one that, as soon as you are rested, we will want you to know about."

Looking again at the portrait, Flower observed he was one most often mistaken for the Lord Christ along with the Master John because, of all the Adepts, these two were most like Him. He further revealed that he was the same one Flower, when a child, knew as the "Promised Prince."

"Until he reveals his name to us," she continued, "we shall call him 'The Brother of Wisdom' for strength and wisdom are what he brings us."

Then thought forms of the most exquisite composition began streaming into her aura. "He said, 'You will recognize my beam and likeness only at those times when you are very still and operating from the center of yourself, on the soul plane. My influence and purpose is to bring you peace and lead you into the Inner Holy of Holies.' "

Flower turned to the others to see their faces, then looked back toward the altar. "Just before his last thought faded out of view," she commented, "he touched his forehead, then placed his hand horizontally across the heart region, and then he placed his hand higher above the heart, fingers pointed upward, I believe to symbolize the Trinity. Next, the glorious voices of the Angels of Adoration and the Angels of Song joined together in praise of this moment. I've never before heard two distinct groups of Angels united in song specifically for an event such as this. It must be," she realized, "because they are as happy as we that this Master has made contact with us and this work."

Flower again looked about the small group who, fifteen minutes earlier, had taken their places in the Chapel for another morning's meditation, unsuspecting of what was to come. Everyone was transformed! Auras were swept clear of their drabness and restless movement; faces shone in wonder. She told them this contact with the Master came about because their prayer work recently had invoked the leadership of the Wise and the Strong and that they would continue to have his help as he had made himself responsible for the work at Questhaven. He also asked that they again be in their places meditating at one o'clock.

For the staff the morning hours passed as if in a dream, so unexpectedly had they been drawn into the orbit of the Master's consciousness and its unaccustomed velocity. What interested Flower, as she went about her duties, was how the Master would proceed in this unique form of instruction. Since Greece, she had known these states of consciousness uninterruptedly. Her teachers, ever since, were her Guardian and these who were the Teachers of Life, the small band of Perfected Men and Women who, having passed through the five gateways of initiation, were now Masters. Everything she taught came from them. What was asked of her, as with every disciple of the Path, was self-conquest, obedience, and mastery of the disciplines given her, first, by incarnated wayshowers and finally, through her own conscious channelship from the inner worlds. Now, with this coming, she was the means of direct contact between the Master and other pupils who lacked her attainments.

Flower and Lawrence meditating in the chapel

By one o'clock everyone was seated, earnestly concentrating on their alignment. The expectant stillness gave way to Flower's words of preparation: "We are again within his beam, his watchfulness, his attention, and we say, "Let the earth receive the impetus from the pure, lofty, and strong consciousness of this Holy One whose disciples we aspire to become."

A moment more of stillness permeated the chapel, then Flower resumed, "Within his beam we sense what tremendous presence of mind he has. It feels as though my whole body has relaxed in him, through his beam. And he says, 'You shall be my watchmen on earth, and since you must testify to Truth, see to it that Truth channels you so that you can verify that to which you testify.' "

For several seconds, no one breathed. Then Flower spoke: "And now his beam is gone and the blue power of the Everliving Christ enfolds us. Like the switching off of a light and the switching on of another, one beam is turned off and the other softer one becomes predominant once again. And this blue beam of healing we ask to bless the whole world, every atom of it, every living creature and person and superman throughout the universe. Every day we especially pray that the light beams from the ones on the lofty levels are given entrance on this sphere to bring us seeds, or possibilities, for determined peace from those who made it work in other worlds."

Later that day, when the Ministry's secretary had typed up copies of the Master's brief message, each individual read and reread his luminous words until they knew them by heart. Was it possible, midway through the twentieth century, to witness such revelation? Were not these words as holy in their origin as any of the sacred books of the world? Think of it! they gasped to themselves, think of it!

The following day when they gathered a few minutes before one o'clock she shared a verse she had been guided to select by the Master for their meditation watchword. It was from Psalms 119:16: "Great peace have they which love thy law; and nothing shall offend them."

"I see his light again today," she said, "as a soft glow instead of the strong beam he sent yesterday. This is just a gentle reminder of his nearness and benediction. He is keeping us in mind, too."

After a moment's silence, she was inspired with the thought, "And the government shall be upon His shoulders— for in some wonderful way this new Master has to do with world peace. To think of Him is to feel one's mind speeding at the rate of a great bullet, Godward! And so be wrapped in peace, and blanketed, enveloped, and protected by Light from the Wise and the Strong who guide and bless the earth."

An atmosphere of electrified speculation hummed in the minds of each one leaving the chapel that afternoon. Would the Master have further word or would He now veil His thoughts for them to apprehend intuitively as best they could? One thing was clear: they had been given at least a glimpse of the consciousness Flower lived in momently—what an awesome experience!

The next morning, at the eight o'clock meditation, Flower began promptly with a description: "I saw what was like a sunrise within the inner planes from afar and it proved to be the Master's soul body. We are in His beam, His words are: 'Find your inner center—the center of your inward selves. When you have found that heart of your real individuality, you will know how to think, how to react, and how to bless those who constitute your present world. Let this be your effort: to keep centered.' "

The Master continued, impressing His thoughts into Flower's aura where she instantly received and translated them: " 'Do not let the pendulum of your route sway too much to the right or left, but hold it poised within and cause its actions to be directed by your spirit will. In other words, permit yourselves only that freedom of action which can be controlled and maintained by your inward self. Let this be your effort this day, and if you will think of me, your Brother in God, I will give you help. I have been with you a long time and shall remain through the rest of your physical years.' "

It was now clear to Flower that the Master intended a new departure for the Work, directly transmitting instruction through her in completed form. It was a venture she would watch with keen attentiveness to evaluate its influence on those receiving its unprecedented baptism.

For everyone it was the beginning of an astonishing dispensation. The messages lengthened in scope, often analyzing aspects of discipleship in surprising detail; other times distilling from enormous complexities the few concentrated sentences that summarized Truth with simplicity and power.

The instruction flowed through with Flower in full consciousness both inwardly and physically. Other Masters frequently were introduced into these meditations, expanding the range of topics and the insight illuminating them. Gradually, two broad themes emerged, encompassing a large majority of the lessons: the disciplines underlying man's quest for God, and esoteric studies of the inner worlds, including a comprehensive description of the Nature and Angel King-

139

doms.

Soon, those attending these meditations, a number that grew rapidly, found themselves deluged with information for which they felt intensely responsible but increasingly unable to apply for lack of hours in the day and the profound sense of their limitations.

What other experience could have better driven home the fact of Flower's place along the Path? All that the Great Ones gave were truths new to her mostly in the form of their statement. The achievements inherent in each of these instructions she had won as a pupil in earlier mystery schools; and everything she taught came to her, then as now, from these identical sources though in the silence and privacy of her unclouded consciousness.

Chapter 12

Trial by Earth

Flower rejoiced at the Masters' coming. It was a bright new departure and its impelling influence on the Questhaven group was gratifying. She carefully listened to the remarks made by the pupils attending the meditations and studied their lives closely for signs of change.

One reaction common to everyone was *wonder*. The experience of extrasensory phenomena, for its own sake, she always had discouraged since it appealed strongly to the personality's fascination with the glamour of secret powers. One of its most dangerous forms, spiritualism, rarely penetrated past the astral plane of the inner worlds and exposed its investigators, at best, to inferior thought patterns; in its worst encounters, it plunged the mind into the blackness of a psychotic abyss. Besides its lower ranges of contact, the medium's loss of consciousness in a trance state surrendered to these obsessive forces the one possession a human rightfully gives only to God—his free will. The risk was an invasion by visions and voices from the purgatories of the astral world, overpowering the victim's mind with what clinically are known as hallucinations.

On the mental plane, contact was of superior quality though still molded by the personality of the recipient. Most of the world's great literature and inspired teachings, she taught, including those attributed to Higher Sources, came from this idealized level, filtering through the archetypal thoughts sent into the earth's atmosphere from Divine Intelligences; and though these fragments were uplifting, they but

Flower and Lawrence around 1950

vaguely resembled the original masterpieces fostering them. Here the compromise, however subtle, was the ego's pride in being so talented and its possessiveness in claiming sole authorship.

Not until a channel is purified of the hold of his or her personality, is contact with inner reality trustworthy, free of the risks permeating phenomena. Before this can happen, the channel must reach the soul level of consciousness—the causal plane.

Many coming to Questhaven on these extraordinary mornings became so enthralled in the event itself they lost sight of an important fact—Flower. All at once they were looking past her, toward the source of her words. If one could listen to Masters, that was the thing! Incredibly, unconsciously, she became to some a means to an end "What would the Master say about that?" was the question defining their new relationship to her. Without realizing the insinuation, they were saying to her, "Flower, go to the Master and get me an answer on this very important matter. Your own judgment has now been superseded "

Flower pondered this development, recognizing the test it presented to her and yet the serious fault it exposed in the pupil. She had not initiated this venture and its course was in the Master's hands, but as a teacher she wanted to find a way of drawing the student's attention to an important oversight.

The following Sunday, fitting these thoughts into a scheduled talk on the attitudes of a disciple, she recalled her own life in Greece during the time of Pythagoras and how many in the audience were with her in those light-filled days Everyone knew of his Academy for it was the famous center of higher learning in the ancient world; they marveled at stories hinting of its mysterious teachings and hungered to share in such knowledge But the instruction was secret and to earn access to it required a degree of spiritual maturity few possessed or were willing to work towards. There was good reason for this: once the pupil entered Pythagoras' school he was made responsible for all Truth revealed to him; how much of the mystery teaching he was ready to assimilate was measured off in the increments of character unfoldment achieved. Of the many present with her today who lived in Greece then, she observed, few chose to make this sacrifice of worldly attachments on which admission rested, and for the few who thought they could, not all succeeded.

The point was clear: in the esoteric schools of the past, no one earned the right of entry who had not first proven himself and taken binding vows to live by everything revealed to him. In the New Age, the conditions were different. For those born into favorable circumstances, access to esoteric Truth came easily. Yet the rule of responsibility held: to be conscious of a Truth and knowingly fail to apply it daily in growing closer to God, incurred an obvious karmic penalty. In subsequent lives the offender would attract circumstances screening out the Light until he deeply, painfully longed for its power to transform his life. Then it would stream into his consciousness again through another channel, in another age, and then at last he would be an apt pupil.

The effect of her sermon was difficult to assess immediately. The mental body, full of curiosity and deft at devouring quantities of information it had neither the intention nor capacity to assimilate, still appeared to account for many attitudes. Others cherished the notion of being one of a chosen few, making of the event a mysterious ritual in which the participation was paramount. Some would have loved to transform these meditations into an elaborate rite, complete with sacred robes, strange symbols, and all the trappings of a clandestine ceremony. Probes or leanings in this direction Flower scattered with warm laughter, reminding them "These are lessons from the Great Ones, not the exercises of a secret cult. What matters is how well we pay attention and learn and how we put these lessons to use in changing our lives."

Then she lifted her face slightly, her eyes glancing over the heads of her listeners, translating inspirations visible only to her, saying "Let's not set ourselves on a pedestal from which we'll surely fall, having failed to live each day giving back to Life the best it has given to us. Don't you see? How much closer that draws us to God and all He has prepared for us than mantrams and gestures!"

And lives did change. To a youth uncertain about his spiritual direction came an answer one morning to an unspoken question. The Master's words electrified him:

My son, it is time, in fact the seasons are over-ripe for your becoming acquainted with Eternity and your finding contact and certainty through it. We want you now to prove yourself to us. When you are ready we can and will prove ourselves to you. We want you, wherever you go, into whatever group, to stand firm. You are to live with valor and with positive attunement to Eternity in all places. You are to remember you have to act for the cause of humanity's advancement this life, and at no time are you free to even indulge any rests or any times of ceasing from such recollections. There are prizes and you will earn them; there are harvests and you will gain them when once you are true.

Within a year he was ordained, committing his life to the service of the Cause along with Flower, Lawrence, and one other minister commissioned during the years of World War II.

For the next several years the lessons continued, sometimes regularly, at other times intermittently, amassing a file of esoteric instruction that, added to Flower's extensive writings previously channeled from these sources, assured a future of inexhaustible study and inspiration.

With the chapel completed and larger numbers of people attending the local services, Flower and Lawrence no longer undertook tours as extensive as those in the thirties and forties.

Except for brief lecture engagements in major cities, their whole effort went into building the Retreat and its training program. The annual pilgrimages were held at Questhaven now and the number of visitors who came to spend a weekend or longer in retreat and study, greatly increased. Its founders had a full-time responsibility right at home.

The outside world also began to stir in ways that meant new problems to be solved, new skills to be acquired and hidden strengths to be found. The first of these experiences involved a wealthy property owner, Mr. A., whose land bordered Questhaven on the north. One of his parcels contained a valley that, at the time, was accessible only by driving his car through Questhaven, parking near a large oak tree that shaded Flower's little study and marked the future site of the permanent chapel. He then made his way along an ill-defined trail he had fashioned to reach his destination a quarter of a mile distant.

Outwardly, he was a cultured, cordial Easterner who periodically dropped in to visit pleasantly, sometimes asking permission to use the trail to his property. He expressed a definite interest in Flower and Lawrence and their work, praising them for a fine pioneering spirit and assuring them of his pleasure in being neighbors.

Then one day he inquired about obtaining a right-of-way across Questhaven to his valley. Not expecting this request, they promised him an answer later but Flower intuitively sensed this would be unwise. The more they thought of it, the more troublesome it became. What guarantee would they have that this right-of-way wouldn't compromise the Retreat's purpose? And, once granted, what if Mr. A., who might be an exemplary neighbor, sold or deeded his property to someone less understanding? Gently, they explained the dedicated status of Questhaven when he happened by on his next visit, counting on his friendly nature to accept their denial gracefully. Instead, his face clouded over and, returning abruptly to his car, he drove away without a word of farewell.

It was several weeks before they saw him again. Then early one morning in April, 1953, from El Cielito, their new hilltop home of a few months, Flower heard an unfamiliar and alarming noise. Running down the hill, she saw a large bulldozer followed by a car containing five men and a dog, boldly headed for the clearing by the large oak and her study.

"Who are you and by what right are you crossing private property?" she demanded. The men looked straight ahead, intent on ignoring her challenge. She recognized Mr. A. behind the wheel of the car, and one of his employees was the operator of the bulldozer. Whatever their plan, it was an outrageous, hostile act that must be stopped.

Lawrence had left an hour earlier on some errands in town. Flower and others on the grounds hurrying to investigate the commotion, after fruitlessly ordering the invaders to stop, could scarcely believe their eyes to see the monstrous machine start carving out a road in the direction of Mr. A's boundary. As the thick stands of chaparral crashed before its blade, growth that was fifteen feet high and fifty years old, no one dreamed there could be any doubt that Mr. A., on this bizarre morning, was constructing a road across Questhaven

146

property, in brazen defiance of another's property rights, the consequences of which he would soon face in a court of law.

Midway through the ordeal Lawrence arrived, dumbfounded by what he saw. At first he reasoned with Mr. A., then he pleaded, finally he threatened to have him arrested. Nothing prevailed. The graying, one-time banker had changed to a personality they'd never seen before. He now was an arrogant, mocking adversary, alternately ignoring and insulting Lawrence, then Flower, and anyone else who challenged him. His eyes were wild in appearance, fiercely set on a goal that seemed incontestably self-incriminating: trespassing on private land to forcibly build an unauthorized road.

Lawrence could do but one thing: drive to Vista and bring back the sheriff's deputy to have him arrested. When they returned, the bulldozer had finished its rape of the canyon and Mr. A. was taken into custody, finally to be released on bail, pending litigation.

When the emotion of this drama calmed, a lawsuit was filled to establish guilt and recover damages. The preliminary legal sparring went along routinely, then suddenly stumbled up against a nightmarish scheme: the defendant would claim he was not trespassing as charged, but merely "improving an existing road" that he had regularly used during the four and a half years he'd owned the property. He would then file a countersuit for obstruction of his right-of-way, false arrest, and damage to his reputation.

Lawrence, when informed of this development, looked at their lawyer incredulously: that was a bald-faced lie! What court would listen to such preposterous nonsense?

The lawyer shook his head ominously. Unless Questhaven could prove Mr. A. didn't have such a road, nor had there ever been a right-of-way on that part of the property in the previous fifty to sixty years, there was a real danger he could win the case on a legal technicality.

What a sinister twist of the facts—instead of the innocent victims, Flower and Lawrence found themselves carrying the burden of proof against their own implied "guilt." It was a chilling trick conceived by a cunning mind, likely before the bulldozer ever destroyed the one piece of evidence standing in its path: the barrier of dense chaparral, a quarter of a mile deep and half a century old. The risk was plain: to lose this battle meant Questhaven would be at the mercy of a triumphant adversary who controlled a road bisecting its principal area and who, in turn, would sue them for heavy damages. All at once the entire future of the Retreat hung in jeopardy. Was it worth such an all-or-nothing risk or should they negotiate for a settlement?

The latter thought never entered Flower's mind. "We are 100% in the right," she said with fire in her eyes, "and we will fight this man all the way to the supreme court of the land, if we must." Her voice was steady and sounded with an authority none had ever heard before. "Wherever the Light is revered," she continued, "darkness will test man's strength to uphold it. In this individual's ruthless effort to wrest from us what he covets for himself, he is our tester. We must keep faith with the source of our strength and face him fearlessly. Where evil is concerned, there can be no compromise. We must fight every foot of the way for total victory."

In the pretrial research, a revealing pattern emerged. Mr. A. on numerous other occasions had been embroiled in similar lawsuits. In all of these encounters he never lost, either gaining the judge's verdict outright or settling out of court in his favor. It was the history of a sophisticated grasp of legal technicalities and intimidation through threats of costly legal action. His bold strike against Flower and Lawrence appeared to be based on the premise that two such gentle, trusting people hadn't the backbone for a real fight and would quickly capitulate, once he had them on the run. How wrong he was!

148

The two he mistook for lambs turned out to be lions, and the battle was joined.

Lawrence spent months tracking down eyewitnesses to testify that no right-of-way had existed in the disputed area in the past sixty years and the present road indeed had been carved by Mr. A's bulldozer. When the case finally reached court in the fall the presiding judge threatened to throw it out in the middle of the second day as no contest, so clearly in the wrong was the defendant. Wishing, however, to have no loopholes for an appeal on technical grounds, the judge allowed Mr. A. to continue his case which promptly descended into an attempt to ridicule and discredit Flower and Lawrence personally, making fun of her teachings about Angels and maligning Lawrence's integrity and manhood. It fizzled shamefully.

When all the evidence was in and closing arguments were finished, the judge upbraided Mr. A. for his unwarranted attacks on the character of Flower and Lawrence and his flagrant disregard of their property rights. As a warning to any future trespassers with similar motives, a fine point of law allowed him to impose triple damages since the chaparral included specimens technically classified as trees. He then served a permanent injunction against the defendant's ever entering Questhaven again. The victory was uncompromising and complete.

Questhaven Retreat around 1950

Chapter 13

The Teaching and Building of Questhaven

The trial and all the incidents leading up to it brought to the surface in the Retreat's founders what few people ever had occasion to see—their warrior spirits. Even those who thought they knew them best were taken aback by the sudden appearance of unshakable courage and the readiness to do battle, whatever the odds, for the Light. It was marvelous; a brilliant lesson in meeting the attack of a calculating, formidable foe unvanquished until this match. Underneath its peaceful beauty, a new strength invested Questhaven.

One question puzzled many of the observers throughout this testing: why hadn't Flower recognized the danger this man posed from their first meeting and why, through her Guardian or her access to the Akashic Records, hadn't she received exact knowledge of his scheme in advance?

The answer was illuminating. The human personality is unpredictable, even to the Higher Ones who examine its every fiber. Anyone, including Mr. A., has the potential for good or evil at any time. To have suspected him initially meant suspecting everyone else coming to Questhaven as a possible enemy of its work. While there is an element of truth in this, no one being the conqueror of his lower nature until mastery, if practiced, it would become an unhealthy form of paranoia. Her training, she explained, is to approach each individual she meets openly until they prove themselves unworthy of this trust. Unless persons are given the opportunity to unfold their best, where is one's faith in their capacity for the Good? And for every Mr. A., there are a hundred, when given this trust, who discover in themselves hidden potentialities never before realized.

As for detailed warnings of impending tests, clairvoyance doesn't always serve to unmask them, but perhaps only to meet them at the best angle of attack, once there is an encounter. This restriction increases the closer the test comes to the life of a channel. It is the growing tip of her own unfinished character, where, in the absence of final answers, she must exercise the necessary faith and resourcefulness to bring about a successful conclusion. Only in this way could she meet her own testings and merit growth.

The expense of the trial had cut heavily into the general fund on which they depended for a surplus to construct future buildings. In securing Questhaven against the land predator they now faced a delay in realizing their permanent chapel, though it was a vital sacrifice. Crowds on Sundays were already overflowing the seating capacity of the small adobe chapel.

Flower never had been finer. Her sermons and classes were alive with new perspectives like vantage points from a peak just surmounted. Most ministers facing the same congregation year after year eventually run out of material, a problem orthodox churches solve by periodically rotating their clergy between parishes. She often spoke on the same subject a half dozen or more times with many people sitting in the audience who had heard each previous version, but never could they recall having heard before this particular approach or these fresh ideas or the examples she used to illustrate her points. She was superbly creative. People often came to hear her on a favorite topic, hoping to recapture the earlier experience; they always left disappointed they hadn't taken better notes the first time yet thrilled not to have missed this latest expression. Her mind was like a stream rising from the snowy heights of a great mountain, ever moving with sweet, clear water, but never the same water, giving life to the thirsty climbers who followed after her.

Her manner reflected the eternal presence of her soul, neither yielding to moods nor donning roles, yet touched by the ever-changing sunlight of illumination. On a particular Sunday morning after the trial she spoke on the major initiations humanity must pass through in their return to God. Her face shone with a soft light which frequently blossomed into full radiant smiles, her eyes sparkling and her lips apart, ready to

Flower A. Newhouse around 1950

share the gladness springing up within her. As she spoke, she supported each point with the feeling it inspired, many times becoming earnest and challenging with fire in her eyes and lightning strikes in her words to signal a danger or awaken a complacent listener. She stood erect and mostly stationary, occasionally shifting her position to include persons in her gaze hidden behind others, always looking directly, deeply into their eyes. Her voice was naturally soft and musical, her tone genuine and sure. She gestured often with her hands forming rounded movements with graceful sweeps and the way she placed them every gesture imparted a benediction.

Her words were formed carefully, her lips never lazy or hesitant. Calling upon an exceptional vocabulary that linked words together effortlessly, she spoke slowly and distinctly, giving potency and meaning to all she said. And when a thought was being impressed upon her, or its expression needed to be just so, she slanted her face upwards slightly while her eyes studied the superphysical dimensions overhead, precisely extracting the essence of its blossoming archetype. At such moments, she often raised her hand, left or right, fingers spread and palm outward, giving to the audience of the light she knew so visibly.

Her lesson that morning described in new language the ancient gateways to human perfection. The first initiation was called the *Birth*—a joyous discovery of the inner side of life giving pupils a deathless imprint of Divinity ever drawing them back to the center where their illumination blazed. It brought the spiritualizing of their life, gaining the control of their senses, emotions and mind. The second initiation was the *Baptism of Fire*, requiring the pupils to overcome fear of the unknown and awakening them to courage, humility, and a disciplined will. The third initiation was known as the *Transfiguration*, bringing the pupils to purity. Of all the

gateways, this one was most transcendent, opening the pupil's eyes to the inner worlds and giving to life an unbroken transparency. It necessitated initiative, boldness, and self-sacrifice.

Then came the most severe threshold, the fourth initiation, inwardly called the *Crucifixion*. When achieved, it gave the candidates the feeling they were being consumed by living fire, demanding complete self-sacrifice, fearless daring, the renunciation and conquest of all evil, and untiring steadfastness. Those passing its trial seldom were popular people in their times since they told the

Flower A. Newhouse around 1954

154

truth as it was. Albert Schweitzer, Mahatma Gandhi, and Abraham Lincoln were of this rank.

The fifth initiation was *Mastery*: the conquest of every deterrent clinging to the candidates, leaving them at last Adepts, a member of the Hierarchy of Perfected Men and Women responsible for the inner government of humanity. Beyond this pinnacle rose the sixth initiation, the Everest of *Lordship*, first conquered by the Christ and making Him Lord of Angels and of Humankind. Too luminous for a human's consciousness to comprehend was the realm of the seventh initiation—Godhood, when each person truly would become one with their Creator.

As 1953 came to an end, the pace of their workload was staggering. Flower looked back through her records to find she had given a total of 88 lectures, 432 interviews and written over 800 letters, mostly in answer to personal needs. Lawrence was equally prolific in his correspondence and counted it his busiest year in office responsibilities, publishing commitments, and Questhaven improvements; and on top of all this, came the many exhausting weeks of detective work in preparing their court case.

In the occasional spaces between their duties, Flower and Lawrence found delightful moments of renewal. They read, painted, watched television, and regularly took long walks in the late afternoon with their family of pets. There were six now: two lovable dogs; Valiant, a red Doberman pinscher; and Frolic, a white Sealyham. Four cats rounded out the animal safari: Darshan, an Abyssinian; Ling, a Siamese; Meliya, a Russian blue; and Anyee, a Burmese. While the "children" explored the endlessly alluring nooks and crannies of nature, Flower was busy gathering armloads of dried grasses and weeds to be dyed and gilded, then arranged in lovely bouquets and given to friends. Once when she and Lawrence both were struggling to manage the unwieldy masses of this-

Flower out for a walk with her pets

tles, seed pods, and feathery spears, the thought of such a ri-
diculous sight sent them into convulsions of laughter. Tears
running down their faces, they gasped for breath, looked at
each other again only to be seized by another fit of laughter
at such an uproarious spectacle. It was a side to their nature
not often seen on the lecture platform, offering them more re-
laxation than a long afternoon nap, and a great deal more fun.

About El Cielito, their home, they soon had six bird baths
and two bountiful feeders. Birds flocked into their yard and
encircled their house, broadcasting their lovely chirps and
trills with scarcely an interruption from dawn to dark. Quail
by the hundreds slipped out of the underbrush, soundlessly
infiltrating the open areas all the way up to the walks to find
kernels of cracked corn Flower and Lawrence kept scattered
about the ground.

There was no limit to the store of love they gave to life in
all its forms and nothing suffered neglect in the radius of this
outreaching. Yet one longing remained unfulfilled for Flower:
children. As busy as they were, as far-ranging as the work
had become, she felt a deep desire for little ones under her

156

own roof to watch over, care for, and guide into the stream of life. Lawrence, looking at the mounting workload and the few hours of precious time they now enjoyed together, set her wish aside as a pleasant but impractical dream.

By the early part of 1956 he had achieved two more milestones in Questhaven's development. All but one mile of the dirt road to the Retreat had been paved and, in the previous year, an earthen dam was erected in the canyon north of the permanent Chapel site. Funds also were being raised for this eagerly-awaited building and, to speed its reality, they had chosen its name: *The Chapel of the Holy Quest.*

One other event made it seem near. Flower had written a detailed description of the Lord Emmanuel as she remembered him in Palestine, sending it to Arthur Learned, the New England artist from whom they had already purchased the original portrait of the Master who came in 1950, along with three others. She wanted a portrait of the Christ, true to His likeness in that life, to place in the new chapel—and it had arrived.

The unveiling, just before the Christmas season, was a breathtaking occasion. Gathering in the adobe chapel, Lawrence carefully unwrapped the protective layers of packing and removed the heavy frame containing the painting. He gently placed it in front of the altar and sat down next to Flower. An expression of nostalgic wonder lighted her face.

"Here it is!" she exclaimed softly. "This is it!"

She paused for a moment to drink in its baptism. "Look at those eyes. Every other picture of the Christ I've seen has failed him there—none ever have had the power to change a life. But look at these! They are the eyes of his soul and just wait and see, they will change lives, ours included."

No other gift could have brought Christmas nearer its inner reality than this. It unveiled an impression of what clairvoyance beholds at such a time—how the continuity of

Life dissolves past and future into an eternal now filled with the presence of the Living Christ. Looking at His face, one's sense of time vanished; nearly two thousand years fell away and suddenly He was here, the Light from His eyes christening the very atmosphere and impelling whoever looked into them to new life.

Chapter 14

Flower, the Counselor

Sundays were work days for Flower and Lawrence. One or the other was up by five in the morning to make final preparations for the day's sermon. Following the service, Lawrence mingled with the congregation, welcoming newcomers, greeting others, and talking with anyone who wished a word with him. Most enjoyed the home-cooked luncheon some of the women provided on the shaded terraces near the old stone dwelling that had been Flower and Lawrence's home for twelve years and now served as the Retreat's office. He passed from table to table, spreading the radiance of his wonderful smile—and if there was a problem, he found time to listen with deep interest, giving his thoughtful advice about what to do.

Sunday afternoons for Flower were stacked with several hours of interviews, a task she handled in a manner all her own. She was entirely purposeful in her attitude toward the one seeking help, relying on her clairvoyance and intuition for the answers. She saw little to be gained in wordiness; her method was not a talking-out therapy allowing the subject to grope for his own perception of the problem, but a teacher-pupil enterprise in which a problem was defined and an answer or a plan of action given. Its prerequisite was teachableness, a factor emphasized by the brief half-hour period allotted for each counseling session. If the interviewee had a strong ego and was grossly self-centered, the thirty minutes were consumed in a one-sided conversation listing a dreary conglomeration of details without once pausing for her reaction. When her secretary's rap at the door indicated it was time for the next interview, the startled talker would protest that she hadn't given an answer to the problem. Flower then would say, "I'm sorry, but you seemed to have a need to do the talking today." If such persons returned for further help, they did so having learned a valuable lesson in the importance of stating the problem in its essentials, then, with pencil and paper in hand, listening attentively.

In interview work, Flower herself listened observantly, waiting for key phrases that pinpointed the salient needs. Often, what she selected as significant had no bearing on the reason for the person's coming originally, but she always aimed at the heart of the true problem. As a teacher, she had a karmic obligation to deal truthfully and directly with spiritual inquiries. Failing to do that would cause her to enter into the pupil's own ring of karma, an error she scrupulously avoided.

For those about whom she cared greatly, who aspired to be disciples of the Path, she used the strongest and most direct words in her vocabulary to break through the indifference, insensitivity, pride, or self-pity entrapping them. Once their blindness was penetrated by the light of this spiritual surgery, her irrepressible love for them swept in to heal the wound and lead them out through the opening of the new perspective.

Some of her interviews of this nature happened unexpectedly, when meeting friends on the grounds of Questhaven or while shopping in town. A woman who was a devoted pupil but introverted, sensitive, and self-bound, constantly bringing up her personal faults to others, met her in the post office one day and immediately began to apologize for some minor shortcoming.

"Marie," commanded Flower, "the trouble with you is you see your mistakes and feel sorry for them. You enjoy self-pity!"

160

A look of hurt and amazement appeared on Marie's face, but for the first time in her life she saw herself as she was to others, and within days a new quality of joy sparkled in her eyes.

Occasionally in an interview her clairvoyance flashed through scenes from the past that explained problems of inscrutable magnitude to ordinary eyes. A couple brought their five-year-old son who had a frightening habit: while at play with other children he many times had tried to strangle them. Recently he was caught placing a noose around another child's neck and might actually have hanged him had the other child's screams not summoned help. A psychologist had explained to them the mechanism of frustration-aggression patterns, though they were still at a loss to isolate the source of these feelings.

When Flower looked at the boy she saw how, as a Portuguese sailor in his previous life, he had been hanged for a crime he hadn't committed. He died furiously protesting what was being done to him and this trauma carried over into his present emotional body, finding an outlet in the compulsive act of inflicting on someone else the punishment that shouldn't have been his. The only permanent release he could expect from this obsession was through receiving love greater than his resentment, and, when old enough to understand, to be told of his past.

Another family, with an equally obscure affliction, knew an instantaneous healing through her clairvoyance. The problem involved a father and mother and their son, third among four boys in the family. The boy was seventeen now, but as long as the mother could remember there had been an unaccountable hatred between this youth and his father. Because they were both fine individuals whom she loved deeply, this unresolved animosity was breaking the mother's heart. Even psychiatrists had failed to understand this puzzling relationship.

As the parents, who were theosophists, finished telling Flower this strange situation, she grew still for a moment; then from the Akashic Records came an illuminating vision. The scene was of Italy many centuries ago. The mother and father, in this other life, were engaged to be married; he was the older and both were members of prominent families. Secretly, however, she was in love with a younger man from a lower social station, a man who in the present incarnation was their son. Since her family would never grant permission to marry him, just before the scheduled wedding to her fiancée, they eloped and ran away to a distant part of the country.

The jilted man, never ceasing to love her, searched from one end of the country to the other until he found them. By now the young couple had fallen into poverty and the woman's health was failing. When he saw what had become of his beloved, the older man turned on the youth he blamed for this outrage, killing him in violent anger. The distraught woman soon died of a broken heart and the wealthy murderer spent several years in prison, then the duration of his life in lonely, straitened circumstances.

When she recounted these events to the astonished parents, they invited their son into Flower's study to hear the story for himself. He listened incredulously at first, then a look of realization came into his face and the three left. Later, Flower received a letter from the mother with the heartwarming news that the father and son, overnight, had become the best of friends now that the mysterious karmic wall separating them had been pulled down.

One Sunday, during her last interview for the day, a woman was seeking help for a marriage now threatened by her unreasoning fear of pregnancy. Flower had recently read an article in the Reader's Digest about an Oregon farmer named Harry Holt who had adopted several Korean-American orphans and now was donating the remainder of his life to finding homes for these war-forsaken children. She urged this desperate wife to consider adopting two of these Amerasian children, a boy and a girl. The woman rejoiced over the suggestion, anticipating her husband's approval, which later was given.

Leaving the interview and walking up the hill to El Cielito, an extraordinary realization came to Flower. She entered their home and said, "Lawrence, you know what we're going to do? We're going to adopt two Korean-American children!"

He looked searchingly into her face, then sank back in his chair convinced of her certainty. It was settled. Whatever lay ahead, the impossible dream was about to come true: Slowly, all of his reservations yielded to the picture before his eyes of his wife's arms filled with a laughing baby girl and, in his own, a smiling boy.

Chapter 15

Adopting Children from Korea

What Flower and Lawrence were about to do meant a sweeping reorganization of their lives. They needed time to think through these changes and they spent a week in the Sequoia National Forest taking with them three books of children's names. When all the balloting was in, it was to be "Galen Keith" and "Melodie Athene". The news caught their Questhaven following completely by surprise. Flower and Lawrence? Adopting children? But how could they? Some shook their heads in bewilderment, never understanding why two people with all they had to do should further complicate their lives with, of all things and at their age, tiny children from an alien land and mixed with another race. Experienced mothers blessed the announcement outwardly but privately suspected Flower had little idea of what lay ahead. Only time would tell.

Then a telephone call to Mr. Holt at his farm in Creswell, Oregon brought a disconcerting answer: for the one hundred or so children waiting at his orphanage headquarters in Seoul, Korea to be officially processed and adopted, there were over two thousand requests. The waiting list suddenly had fallen years behind the supply with the appearance of the Reader's Digest article. What were they to do?

Flower then recalled the three Adams brothers who visited Questhaven from time to time when on furlough from their duties as missionaries in Korea. She urged Lawrence to write them, asking what could be done. The answer came promptly: his best chance was to come to South Korea personally and locate children by driving through the numerous villages near Seoul.

When Mr. Holt heard of this plan he urged Lawrence not to make such an expensive trip on his own. The obstacles against getting children home, even if he located them, probably would prove insurmountable. Earlier encouragement from the International Social Service also cooled rapidly. If the trip were to be taken, it would have to be taken on faith alone, as had everything else of value in their lives. To cover its cost they withdrew much of their savings and Lawrence lost no time preparing for his journey. Then two other families in the Questhaven group joined the founders asking him to find either a boy or girl. By flight time he was hoping to locate four children.

Korea in early September of 1956 stirred Lawrence with the mystic beauty of its hills and the dignity of its people though his sight-seeing was limited to the countryside between one address and another in pursuit of his goal. And on that matter, frustration hounded him. American officials were of little help, even to the point of advising him he'd come on a wild goose chase; the Koreans were slow to move. Much of the time there were no telephone operators on duty and he discovered he could cross the city of Seoul and find his party faster than waiting to complete a call. The weather was already bitter cold. At night he put on every item of clothing he possessed and still couldn't keep warm. But the most discouraging development was his fruitless search for children. Wherever he went, none appeared and the leads given him all proved false. Were the embassy officials right? Had he come such a distance to return empty handed? The thought haunted him sporadically, especially at the end of an exhausting day, and he fervently wished to see it dispelled by the sight of the first eligible child.

The Adams brothers worked in and about Seoul, and it

now appeared the area had turned over most of its Korean-American children to Harry Holt's program. When Lawrence reported his lack of success to Flower one evening on an overseas call her intuition directed

Gathering supplies in Korea

him to go south of the capital. In discussing this plan with the two brothers, they gave him the address of a Reverend and Mrs. Provost, a missionary couple in Pusan, about a day's journey from Seoul along the coastline overlooking the entrance to the Sea of Japan. Mrs. Provost, they said, spoke fluent Korean and would be willing to go with him into the outlying villages where such children frequently had been seen.

Renting a jeep, he went immediately to Pusan and the next day, joined by this gracious woman, renewed the search. In and out of the farms and villages they drove, at last seeing the half-American, half-Korean youngsters peeking out from behind buildings, other times hearing of them from an observant villager. But they seldom were seen at play with the all-Korean children. His hostess explained that the Korean society, as with other oriental cultures, looked upon fatherless children of mixed race almost with the same rejection as had India towards its untouchables, placing them at the bottom of a rigid social order. Their future was permanently blighted by this fact, exposing them to beatings and hateful ridicule as they grew old enough to want to play with other children. By the end of their journey Lawrence was an eyewitness to several stonings whose targets were the children for whom he hunted. And the mothers, as long as they carried this stigma, couldn't find husbands or decent employment. When the children were between one and two years old, many of these mothers saw the hopelessness of their child's future and their own; as news slowly got around that American parents were eager to adopt these youngsters, offering them good homes and the promise of a normal life, the distraught women reluctantly brought them to the Americans they'd learned to trust: the missionaries. The children they sought now, however, were in remote rural communities where no missionaries lived.

Nothing came easily, but at last they were finding children. On one of these expeditions everything had gone wrong. It was the season of heavy rains and there were no bridges over the streams separating the villages. The jeep had to ford swollen streams, frequently getting stuck half way across or sinking to its hub caps in the mire on either side. After having nearly all of his film ruined by the floodwaters and losing several hours of daylight, they struggled into a small village where he found a half-starved Korean-American boy with a shy, winning smile. Watching the little fellow devour all the food handed to him, it suddenly came to him this thin wisp of a lad was their Galen. Had it not been for the annoying delays at the river crossing they would have missed him altogether.

Stopping at a checkpoint

Within a few days Lawrence found himself the guardian of twenty frightened, fascinated, adorable

168

children, including a beautiful girl, irrepressibly curious and lovable named Melodie. Upon finding her, the mother was so impressed with the integrity of this American who had travelled halfway around the world to become a father, she led him to a friend who also was willing to give up her Korean-American daughter for the assurance of a happier future.

The next problem was what to do with them.

❧ ✳ ☙

The next morning Lawrence looked around him. The twenty children lay sound asleep in makeshift beds throughout the missionary's home, for the moment oblivious to the change the last few hours had wrought in their lives. He studied each of their faces with the loving adoration of a father towards his firstborn. What a surprise awaited them - a whole new world from top to bottom, inside and out, and he would witness this metamorphosis each thrilling step of the way.

It was now clear what had to be done. He learned in a phone conversation with Flower that other parents in the Questhaven family, realizing the once-in-a-lifetime opportunity Lawrence represented, now wished to adopt children. This left him with the practical problem, not only of providing for them, but of finding a way to legally process their adoptions and to gain their admission as aliens into the United States. The International Social Service offered little hope for assistance since their program was both slow and provided for a mere handful of youngsters. Only Mr. Holt's headquarters in Seoul was set up to handle this problem realistically. Remembering the long waiting list of prospective parents at the Holt orphanage, Lawrence returned to the South Korean capital and made them an offer: If they would process the ten children he needed for his own commitments, they could place the remaining ten into homes on their waiting list.

The arrangement was gladly accepted and the next day he arrived with his little band of wide-eyed Amerasians. Lack of space at their limited facilities made it necessary to house the children at the nearby Seoul Clinic, another philanthropic organization operated by a Los Angeles bible minister. As Lawrence walked through the door, he heard a voice call out to him "Aboji, aboji!"

He knew this Korean word for "father" and as he turned to see who was shouting it, a dark-eyed boy about three years old flung his arms around his legs.

"Aboji!" he repeated with a bright smile.

Lawrence was deeply touched by this incident and each day he looked forward to greeting the lad who now tagged at his heels wherever he went. Cho Soo II, as he was called, clearly had claimed Lawrence for his father. Wondering if this was a sign, he made some inquiries which revealed the possibility was out of the question - the youngster long had been slated for adoption by the Clinic's director. After this, Lawrence was careful not to let the relationship go any farther than a friendly companionship, though he could see in Cho Soo's eyes it wasn't ending there.

On Mr. Holt's staff was a young Korean, Hyung Bok Kim, who handled the legal arrangements required in granting the proxy adoptions and obtaining their immigration visas into the United States. Mr. Kim and Lawrence soon became fast friends as they united their talents to conquer the bureaucratic obstacles between the children and their new life in America. It was tedious, frustrating business consuming weeks of precious time before the harsh Korean winter set in and so many of the children would perish for lack of adequate medical care, food, and protection.

Then a remarkable situation developed. The director of the Seoul Clinic was faced with a personal matter forcing him to consider giving up his plans to adopt little Cho Soo

II. Mr. Holt, having heard of Lawrence's attachment to this boy through Mr. Kim, had called to ask if he wished a second son, should the other man abandon his plans. That night Lawrence placed a call to Flower.

"Sweetheart," he began, "you know the little Korean-American boy here at the Seoul Clinic I've written about who adopted me as his 'aboji'?"

"Yes," she answered.

"Well, I've just heard from Mr. Holt that he may become available. What do you think about being the mother of three children?"

"Yes, it's all right with me," she replied, aware that these two shared a bond from other lives and the sudden change in the child's status meant a go-ahead. "What will we give him for a name?"

"How about the other choice on our list," he answered, "Christopher Kevin?"

"Wonderful," she said.

The next decision facing Lawrence was not so simply resolved. The Refugee Relief Act of 1953 wouldn't expire until December of the current year but, except for a final group of twenty-five youngsters already cleared including the delighted Cho Soo, its quota was exhausted and the U. S. consul couldn't grant special visas. Realizing there was nothing more to be done in Seoul, he said farewell to all of his new friends, kissed his many children goodbye, after making every arrangement for their safekeeping, and flew back to California. His last sight of the Seoul Clinic was of little Galen forlornly standing in the doorway watching his daddy's car disappearing down the street.

On the return trip Lawrence joined Mr. Holt's daughter and another woman in shepherding the last load of adopted children to their new homeland. It was a hectic, sleepless flight, but a reward at the end overwhelming him: the sight of the new parents straining to catch a glimpse of their long-awaited children; then one at a time, reaching out to fill their arms with their own. After seeing Cho Soo off to Mr. Holt's farm in Oregon, he arrived at Questhaven exhausted and thin, but with an armload of pictures to distribute to several anxious parents and a head full of fascinating memories to share with everyone. Two days later Mr. Holt telephoned Lawrence that a final decision had been made not to go through with Cho Soo's previous adoption; furthermore, he had been screaming inconsolably for his "aboji." "If you want this boy," Mr. Holt said with unrestrained emphasis, "he's yours. We can't do a thing with him - he just wants you." At long last they were parents indeed. That same day Lawrence flew to Oregon and the Holt farm in Creswell.

Meeting Mr. Holt started a second train of events in motion. The only hope for those left behind in Korea with winter fast approaching was in persuading Congress to increase the quota of the 1953 Refugee Act and extend it for an additional time period. The plain-spoken farmer had little patience with political bottlenecks and asked Lawrence if he would go to Washington D.C. as his personal emissary to plead the orphans' case to anyone who would listen. The situation was gloomy: not only did it require an Act of Congress but the key people whose support was vital were nearly impossible to reach. Other matters of greater national concern crowded the agendas and the Act itself was only meant as temporary relief, certainly never intended to be a loophole to slip through children of Korean mothers fathered by unknown American servicemen. The International Social Service organizations were powerfully opposed to its use on this basis.

Lawrence, as mild-mannered and accommodating as he appeared, always went straight to the top for a cause in which his heart was committed. Through a friend who had a contact near the President, he got an interview with Sherman Adams,

172

Eisenhower's personal advisor, who later took him to lunch in the executive dining room upon hearing his story. By the middle of the afternoon he had the President's okay, virtually assuring congressional passage, and an extraordinary bonus besides. To offset the delay in passing the legislation and to beat the Korean winter, Eisenhower issued a special quota of presidential visas enough to bring over all the stranded children. Lawrence also met with several congressmen who gladly pledged their support, and representatives of the State Department and the Immigration Service, but this was anti-climactic. The unlikely breakthrough had been realized in the stunningly short span of a few hours. When he later received the news by phone, Mr. Holt was speechless with gratitude; impressed by Lawrence's deep sincerity he was unprepared for his swift success. He thought he'd sent a man dedicated enough to pace the halls of Congress tirelessly with the slim hope of turning a resistant tide of apathy. Instead, he'd commis-

Newly arrived in America

sioned a knight on a bold charger before whom the gates of the White House swung apart.

For Flower and Lawrence there was a personal dividend to this achievement - Galen and Melodie would now be home for Christmas. On December 16th, a chartered Pan American DC 7 carrying ninety-one Korean-American children landed at San Francisco. A weary Mr. Holt emerged from the cabin handing Melodie to Flower, saying, "Here's your little girl." Galen followed by a few minutes in the arms of a friend.

Flower was ecstatic. Lawrence beamed with the joy this particular flight meant to him; on board were the twenty children he had personally located, hidden in the remote villages of South Korea—an adventure imperishably stamped into his memory. And now he saw them each in the arms of adoring parents. Then together, after twelve hours of waiting, hugging, bathing little bodies, changing diapers, putting on fresh clothes, and getting a bite to eat, they departed for home and a warmer, busier, brighter life ahead.

What a wonderful new experience began for Questhaven! The usual quiet of their home was traded for the sound of the children's laughter, tears, and endless questions. At first, there was an even exchange between Korean and English but gradually the Korean lost ground to the children's rapid facility to acquire their new language. Food preferences presented a challenge, especially salads which they'd never eaten. To coax them in this direction the imaginative parents spread cashew nut butter on rolled lettuce leaves, calling their creations "Popeye sandwiches" after the children's favorite television cartoon program.

With the passing of the months the personalities of the three youngsters unfolded rapidly. Melodie was the youngest; she was affectionate, curious, quick to learn, and sometimes demanding. Galen was between his brother and sister in age, rather shy and secretive, with a huge smile and a peaceful disposition. Christopher was the oldest; he was active, alert, and outgoing; a good worker but also strong-willed and stubborn with an explosive temper. Lawrence had his hands full in managing the frequent spells of defiance erupting in Christopher but, like everything else, he handled it admirably well. When a crisis was surmounted the boy's happier side blossomed with an eagerness to please that touched his parents deeply.

The coming of the Korean-American children meant for

Questhaven's founders, the other families welcoming their own new arrivals, and the entire following, an upsurge of rejuvenation. It awakened a kinship with humanity touching the true continuity of life across all continents and races; it rediscovered the innocence and wonder of childhood, its pleasure in newness, and its overflowing capacity for love.

Flower's talks now were sprinkled with episodes of parenthood full of humor and wisdom. The Sunday congregations filled the little adobe chapel, spilling over onto the outside veranda. The urgent need was to realize the Chapel of the Holy Quest soon.

Chapter 16

Trial by Water

More than ever, Flower needed the surcharging of the mountains; her doctor became concerned about the mounting pressures in her life and, aware of a congenital heart condition, urged her to slow the pace of activity and find more time for rest. As often as she could—sometimes alone, sometimes with Melodie, and sometimes joined by the entire family—she spent glorious, sunny days in the evergreen fragrance of their Idyllwild home The demands of motherhood, the needs of Questhaven, and the unrelenting schedule of lectures, interviews, correspondence and writing that accelerated each year pressed about her, reaching density levels that would have been suffocating except for these breathing spells of renewal.

About an hour or two before sundown she loved to take walks; along the mountain trails and up abandoned logging roads into areas unfrequented by other hikers. In the stillness of the late afternoon, walking slowly upward, her eyes skimmed the treetops, drinking in the soft, lustrous seas of light rinsing through the silvery pine boughs and cedar branches. Devas would manifest themselves and occasionally a nature Angel or the Lord of the Mountain himself would appear, filling a great piece of the sky with a brilliance of light no sunset or rainbow could rival.

Her delight on these walks was to find nature treasures. A gnarled piece of wood with a rich patina sheen from years of exposure to sun, rain and snow, sweeping up like a wing, she took as a symbol of aspiration; another, with an open knothole represented the single eye of clairvoyance; a glittering stone shaped like a heart with a quartz center, reminded her of the diamond-quality of purest love. A blue feather on the path signified the true way; and a triangular stone, the Trinity. Every walk yielded armloads of these enlightening finds and the best ones were carefully brought back to be placed in a growing collection of nature revelations.

Two projects protruded above the thick forest of work surrounding Lawrence at the Retreat: a new chapel and a new well. Funds had nearly reached the goal for the former. An architect had been retained and the site surveyed and graded. The search for additional water had brought to Questhaven a remarkable German-educated geologist with an uncanny reputation for locating productive wells in arid terrain.

Proceeding from a theory postulating two kinds of water—"secondary" or surface water which seeps down through the porous layers of earth, and "primary" water which is formed deep in the earth's interior finding its way up through fissures and faults toward the surface—he located a well site on a single day's visit and assured them this would more than meet their foreseeable needs. The drilling depth was set for between five and six hundred feet, a goal never reached because of a frustrating series of broken drill heads. But the two wells, each half complete, already tapped such an abundance of the "secondary" supply, there was no necessity to go farther. Twenty-four hours after the installation of the pump the 165,000 gallon Questhaven reservoir was full for the first time and its future secure. The same year, rains saturated Southern California and the dam, dry since its construction, swelled to overflowing, sending a cascade of splashing water over the spillway and down the canyon. At night an orchestra of frogs and crickets, the like of which Questhaven had never known, played to a full house of encircling hills, chaparral and starry skies.

The opulence of these riches, like jewelry in a showcase, soon brought a new encounter with outside interests—this time a monolithic organization bent on extending its hold over Questhaven's water assets. The largest water district in Southern California, responding to requests of land developers and large property holders in the northern part of San Diego County, was preparing to form a satellite water district which arbitrarily included Questhaven along its northern boundary. If approved by a majority of the area's residents, property owners would finance the new district largely by taxes based on the amount of acreage each possessed. For land speculators it was a boon but to a nature preserve it threatened its very existence.

In achieving a ring of protective hills on nearly all sides, two hundred additional acres had been added to Questhaven in the mid 1950's, bringing its total to 640 acres—a square mile of hills and canyon. Lawrence soon learned that the proposed district not only would bill Questhaven for its share of developmental costs but it would have the power to supersede all of the property's water rights, allowing the acquisition of its existing wells and all future sources of water.

Again an exhaustive search for a solution began and a new legal battle darkened the Retreat's horizon. To fail to be excluded from this water authority meant a devastating financial burden that easily could sap the life flow of support sustaining Questhaven. There was also a dreadful difference between this legal struggle and the previous one: the overwhelming power and financial resources of the new opposition.

When a hearing was held in the principal district's mahogany paneled board room in Los Angeles, an astoundingly cold, ruthless position became clear. For an hour or more, testimony was given before the distracted, cigar-smoking board members, including an appeal to simply draw the boundaries beneath Questhaven, cutting it out of the proposed area altogether. In the middle of a technical debate over the chance of Questhaven having the benefit of seepage from adjacent water district users—an argument nullified by the Retreat's higher elevation relative to the surrounding terrain—one of the group interrupted the exchange to state the board's true position: "It wouldn't make any difference," he said with a cynical smile, "if Questhaven was a bald granite outcropping on the top of a ten thousand foot peak; if the property falls within the water district's boundaries, the owners will pay just like anyone else." He then settled another point, rocking back in his chair, speaking deliberately and with an air of finality. "What's more, the only way you're going to get yourself out of this district will be to defeat it at the polls. Otherwise, you're in."

Lawrence looked at his lawyer who shook his head in disbelief. The prospect of fighting a delaying action in the courts would be impossibly expensive and, in the end, futile. A period of puzzlement set in, but it never turned into despair. Lawrence wrote letters, talked with property owners who had faced similar situations, and counseled again with their lawyer. A lead he'd stumbled upon sometime earlier, then set aside as impractical, suddenly flashed across the night sky with the solution: if Questhaven could form its own official water district first, the lawyer found out it then had the right to vote itself out of any future district planning, such as the proposal in question.

A few months later, the filing and paper work behind them, the residents of Questhaven legally fulfilled the board member's callous prophecy, but in a way he'd never have guessed—defeating the proposed district at the polls by creating their own water agency exactly one week before the deadline set by their rival's schedule.

Triumphs such as this gave Flower, Lawrence and their

large number of supporters a stirring verification of the Retreat's destiny: to be a sanctuary free from the outside world's intrusion, consecrated forever to the Christ. How steadfast was the inner side of life, once the pupil held true!

Plans for the Chapel of the Holy Quest had been completed in the fall of 1958 and sent out to bid. On a day late in December, the bids were slowly, expectantly opened. The results were startling: even the lowest figure was nearly twice the cost given the architect to work within. It was a moment for Lawrence, who put his all in every task but the extra love of creation in this one, to pause and ask his wife, "Sweetheart, why do the things that mean the most to us so often have to come the hard way?"

Flower reflected a little while, then answered, "Because we have to learn through our own experience how to surmount obstacles and build an unshakable foundation for the Work on these acres of the Lord. If the way was cleared for us each time, without forcing us to master new disciplines," she added, "how would we be sure of our strength and our faith? I think this is a lesson for us to plan more simply, to be willing to set aside all of our previous effort, and begin again."

And they did. A new architect was found whose work immediately struck her as both functional and sensitive to the themes they idealized: reverence, simplicity, warmth, and, in the chapel's overall effect, the creation of a window into the inner worlds. By the fall of 1959, the new bid was accepted and construction began. Lawrence, lovingly, tenderly, joyously, oversaw its progress. Every rose-tinted concrete block went into place with his smiling approval. Step by step, he photographed the construction process—the rising walls, the buttresses for the gigantic supporting beams, the altar, the ceiling, the windows stained in solid pastel hues, filtering in the rich sunlight; and finally the long wooden pews and soft beige carpeting.

181

Every Saturday, as the building progressed, he went with a broom to the construction site and carefully swept clean the cluttered concrete floor, straightened the stacks of lumber, and removed the piles of trash so that visitors on Sunday would have the best possible impression of the chapel's unfolding beauty.

The last of the interior furnishings to be set in place was a figure of the Christ commanding the center of the broad altar. Slightly larger than life size, it stood over seven feet tall and was carved out of a great trunk of elm by the distinguished German wood sculptor, Otto Flath. The gentle smile of serenity on His face, the outward spreading arms consecrating the onlooker, the warm glow of sculptured wood bathed in the blending hues of light created by the stained glass panels rising in the background from floor to ceiling, inspired stillness and reverence.

On April 3, 1960, just two weeks before Easter, the chapel was dedicated before a crowd overflowing its three hundred seat capacity. It was a new decade and, for Questhaven, the beginning of a new era.

Chapter 17

Thou Good and Faithful Servant

In the fall the children were back in school. Melodie was now in the first grade, Galen in the second, and Christopher in the third. All remnants of their Korean language and culture had disappeared; Americanization was complete. The heart condition that beset Flower off and on faced her with a decision bluntly stated by the heart specialist she now regularly visited: either slow down or risk a fatal heart attack. The warning spurred Lawrence into action. Her interview schedule must be sharply curtailed, particularly where difficult individuals were involved. Her correspondence load must be reduced to a fraction of the nearly one thousand replies annually leaving her desk. More help with the housekeeping chores and the children also must be arranged. And she must have more time to rest and study in their mountain home. This achieved, she could concentrate the major portions of her energy on lecturing and writing, the two most fertile fields in which to broadcast the seeds of Truth.

The opening of the Chapel of the Holy Quest was like the deepening of a reservoir—overnight the attendance nearly doubled. People coming to Questhaven for the first time, or returning after several years, hardly could believe that such an exquisite creation existed, hidden below the brow of a rising slope, appearing unannounced like a revelation. Discovering it, in a small way, was like the holy quest itself, manifesting when least expected, suddenly imprinting its memory for the remainder of the beholder's life.

The 1960s were to be dramatic years. Already Lawrence

Flower and Lawrence with the sound engineer

was busy gathering ideas for the next building project, a center for fellowship receptions, recitals, art exhibits, classes, and family gatherings. Its name would be Friendship House. Another matter weighing heavily upon him was the need to gain tax exemption for all the Lord's acres at Questhaven, not just the token four acres granted by the tax assessor for roads and building grounds. By the fall of the year another concern commanded attention: the threat to the spiritual foundation of the nation posed by a drift toward atheism, immorality, and a perilous accommodation of international Communism. His first personal encounter with the latter evil occurred in Korea when he listened to rumors spread by red propaganda that children given to missionaries by the anxious Korean mothers were never adopted by American families but dumped into the Pacific to be rid of them. This was the principal reason behind his difficulty in finding children when he first set out.

He swiftly buckled on the armor of his knight's courage and became a champion of his country's rights and responsibilities of God-given citizenship. He was startled by the complacency of people everywhere—even in the congregations in the Chapel of the Holy Quest—to the infestation of the antichrist slowly creeping into the heartwood of the land. As a minister, father. and countryman, he wouldn't rest until he had done everything in his power to oppose this trend and reestablish trust in God as the principal article of faith for nation, church, and home.

In the months ahead he hurled himself into this battle, realizing that Questhaven would have no future if freedom to worship was undermined. Yet he never allowed the intensity of the threat to blind him to his primary disciplines as a spiritual pupil and wayshower. Centeredness—the necessity to keep attuned to the inner worlds—remained his chief effort. It gave him the integrity of his own intuitive channelship and the clear-headed poise of a seasoned warrior. More than ever, he was light-filled and great-hearted; most of all, he was selfless. Wherever he was, whatever he was doing, it was to help Flower, to care for the children, to benefit the Retreat, to uphold the Light. He asked nothing for himself and miraculously seemed to have everything his heart desired: love, work, purpose, fulfillment.

The occasion distilling the purest essences within Lawrence, and his luminous companion, was holy communion on Good Friday. The chapel, filled and hushed, glowed in a soft, crystalline light that seemed to dissolve whatever distraction or restlessness the audience contained. He opened the service by standing in the speaker's podium, pausing to look across the gathering, his face shining and his eyes large and wide awake, intentionally seeking out every face before him. Then, in a voice gentle with humility, he welcomed each one present. Like vapors of incense, reverence emanated from his whole being, permeating the chapel, yet a reverence made warm and vibrant with his marvelous radiance. As one gloriously conscious of what he was about, he sounded the keynotes of the communion experience leading up to his introduction of Flower. Then she took her place in the podium. Something akin to an electric current passed through the chapel just to look at her. Greece, Palestine, and Questhaven all at once seemed to be the same place and the same moment of time. Her boundless love reached out to every worshiper in the meeting of her eyes and the joyousness of her words. From every facet of her presence streamed the awakening flames of consecration. As she spoke, the atmosphere of the chapel changed from solemn reflection to an alert awareness of Christ's momentous immanence, here and now. Every word was like a step closer to the altar; every glance, an inch nearer the window of her clairvoyance.

While she spoke, Lawrence looked upon her, rapt in adoration, absorbing each sentence as the breath of his spiritual life. He was the complete pupil, yet by that reality, a bright wayshower at his beloved's side.

The communion began with a line of celebrants kneeling along the carpeted edge of the altar platform. Flower went first, serving the bread. As she reminded each one of its inner symbolism, she looked straight into their eyes, and for those who returned this blazing recognition a wave of spiritual fire swept through them from the crown of their heads to the soles of their feet. Lawrence followed with the little glasses of juice, pausing to remind each one of its significance. The look of compassion that directed his words made him a brother of spirit to anyone wise enough to give back the same deep realization into his eyes.

Together, Flower and Lawrence were Questhaven. Inseparable in their service and unique in their individual gifts, they shared the single purpose of creating both a retreat and an inner school. She was the architect, the pathfinder and channel, he was the builder, preparing the retreat facilities and tending to the practical details of the Work. Yet, his inner experiences were splendid mystical openings looking out upon Divinity's mystery and she was keenly interested in each of the down-to-earth details he managed. Two such perfectly matched souls founding such a singular enterprise—storm-tested and victorious—having kept the faith, what more would the future bring?

Flower, in all of her previous incarnations, could not recall living past the age of forty. This life, with its enormous demands on her energy, already had outsailed this farthest time line along the shores of her former voyages. It was no simple matter to stay in the earth dimension. The hardship of a physical existence in a body so delicately sensitive to the harsher elements of life often caused her to look up longingly into the visible heaven about her. How easy it would be to step out into its fathomless peace, its unspeakable beauty; not to escape from the density of the one but to return to the ethereal

The Newhouse family during an animal blessing

bliss of the other. It was the yearning of a captive bird for the open skies. Many things prevented this: her commitment to life's mission, Lawrence's companionship, her children, and the thirst of so many—as long as God gave her the strength—to drink from the spring of her channelship.

The bouts with an uncertain heart condition made her conscientious about frequent checkups not only for herself but everyone close to her. She did not agree with presumptuous people who advised her to rely solely on her faith in God or to become an adherent of health foods as the only trustworthy way to health and wholeness. "God's healing power," she reminded them, "is just as available through a surgeon's hands or a physician's prescription as through the food we eat, the hours we rest, or the prayers we raise up to Him. Don't limit the varieties of His dispensation." And to a mind entrenched in the belief of its own power to be the instrument of Divine intervention, she often added, "Be careful it isn't your pride

187

rather than your faith that leads you."

When Lawrence mentioned a discomforting sensation in his chest she promptly insisted he have a thorough examination. Looking at his aura she noticed a darkness in the heart region, needing immediate attention. The report a few days later was guardedly optimistic. The condition should be watched carefully and he should return in six months for another check.

His tempo never slackened, a sign to everyone aware of the examination that, whatever the difficulty, it was already mending. To anyone else, except Flower who took nothing for granted, he was his usual steadfast self, cheerfully filling the hours with the work he loved.

In the spring of 1962 the three Newhouse youngsters were well along in school. An affectionate father, firm in his expectations, Lawrence took great care to establish the traits of character he idealized for each of the children. His bond with Christopher carried over from the past the boy's need not just for love but unswerving discipline. He was like two people; an eager trustworthy helper at his father's side on his good days but a defiant storm center of trouble on those that were bad. The only force capable of stopping him at these times was Lawrence's strong arms. When the confrontation passed, Christopher was reassured that his father's strength exceeded his own rebel willfulness, and love, like a rising sun, still filled the sky of his world with warm light.

The discomfort in his chest had not improved and at the end of the six month period Lawrence's physician sent him to a specialist. To be safe, exploratory chest surgery was scheduled so that cancer could be ruled out and any possible growth investigated. Flower was relieved to hear this was a routine procedure, commonly advised in a case such as Lawrence's, considering the prolonged nature of the discomfort and the good sense of catching things early. The operation meant a period of about four to six weeks of recuperation, raising the practical problem of managing the children and the multitude of daily affairs concerning Questhaven while he rested and regained his strength, but arrangements were promptly made to meet their needs.

At the hospital, everything went smoothly and in less time than they expected the surgery was finished and Lawrence was in the recovery room. A short while later, the surgeon emerged from one of the doors, asking to speak with Flower. His face was sober and strained; he spoke slowly, avoiding alarm yet aware that his words were the last thing she wanted to hear. As kindly yet honestly as he could, he told her what he had found: cancer of the left lung too advanced to be operable. All he could do, after taking a few tissue samples for biopsy, was to sew up Lawrence's chest. The condition, while susceptible to further treatment, was very probably terminal.

Flower stood there, her earthly world collapsing with each word. "Not Lawrence," she said to herself, "not Lawrence. This can't be. The Work needs him. I need him. We all need him." For the moment, all she felt was the numb, sinking sensation of a shock too brutal to comprehend.

As she drove home with friends that day, the finality of the surgeon's words returned again and again to her. "Why does it have to end this way?" she thought. "Why do I have to accept this verdict? There must be a way for Lawrence to be healed; through medical channels, through prayer, somehow must come a miracle from God if it is His Will!"

Sitting up straight, she pledged herself to a fight, the most desperate fight of her life, against the stealthy, venomous invader destroying Lawrence's body cell by cell. She began praying for him as she'd never prayed for anyone or anything in her life. Not an hour of the day passed, nor many within the night, without a request to an inner source for help: the Healing Angels, the Angels of the Christ Presence, the Spirit of Grace, the Spirit of Truth, the Lord Christ, and God, the Mother-Father Spirit of Life. No avenue was overlooked; every promise of hope was tapped.

A few days after the operation a piece of good news came back from the medical laboratory: Lawrence's cancer, though malignant, was of a type that responded well to cobalt treatments. As soon as he had recovered sufficiently from the surgery, these were begun. Flower was no longer alone in this battle for her husband's life. Lawrence met the challenge with the full force of his will. From the beginning, when he first received the news, a light flashed in his eyes that signaled he'd never surrender. Somehow, by whatever strength and discipline God asked of him, he would conquer this enemy. A series of 24-hour prayer vigils began, sponsored by those who knew and loved Lawrence, many in cities as far away as New York.

The results were astonishing—miraculous. Though the cobalt treatments produced the only severe pain Lawrence suffered, the cancer atrophied as if touched by a magic wand. Within weeks his x-rays were clear and all tests of persisting cancer ruled negative. The vitality slowly seeped back into his limbs and the day came when the doctor, incredulous at Lawrence's response, released him from further therapy, scheduling him for a routine postoperative check in four months.

On the Sunday morning when he returned to the lecture platform, his face thinner and his body still recovering from the effects of his ordeal, he read the twenty-third psalm, pronouncing each word with great care. When he finished, he closed the Bible, remembering aloud how many times he'd heard this eloquent psalm without comprehending its true message. "Now I know what it means," he said, his eyes moist with feeling, "for I have stood in the valley of the shadow of death," and in his voice was the unmistakable tone of certainty that comes from direct knowledge alone. A new humility possessed him. It was a quality he'd never lacked but the difference was the deep sense of earnest reverence for the gift of life that now replaced his lighthearted, unassuming reflection of this quality in previous years.

Throughout the unbelievable weeks of Lawrence's affliction the most startling thing had been that it was happening at all and to him. Flower was the one who seemed tenuously anchored to her body, whose heart might falter in the journey across the middle years of life. But Lawrence stood at her side like a giant sequoia. His sturdiness promised to be the difference for her, adding precious years to her mission. Surely that was the plan of the Higher Ones—their way of undergirding her uncertain physical vehicle.

The unforeseen likelihood of his own death shook the complacency others had attached to his well-being. Many had faced the possibility of Flower's return into Eternity ahead of Lawrence; none for a moment, until this blow fell, considered it the other way around. And now the entire episode was past, like a frightening dream. Awakened, the dreamer could learn never again to take such an expectation for granted and to place upon Lawrence a new valuation.

Plans were made to travel to New York for a week of lectures in the fall. It was the first major trip of this kind Flower and Lawrence had taken together for three years and Melodie would accompany them. Summer that year became a celebration of many things: his return from the brink of death; the start, in a small way, of their daughter's participation in speaking the word; and restorative powers of the mountains as they spent long days at their Idyllwild hideaway, gathering in renewal to fill the depletion exacted by the last several weeks.

Then it happened, like the descent of an arctic wind out of season paralyzing what moments before was a clear, warm, pleasant day. The cancer returned. Worst of all, when the laboratory tests were completed, they revealed the flare-up this time in the lymph system, spreading its merciless grip throughout Lawrence's body. The medical language was chillingly unambiguous and unyielding: condition terminal. A few weeks; at most, perhaps three months, and he would be gone. He refused to hear of it. Without closing his eyes to the stark statistical chances against another miracle, he prepared himself to renew the battle. He began by joining forces with his wife, the two of them praying together, using every metaphysical and esoteric technique known, day after day. Flower sought help from the inner worlds, going to every higher presence known to her, but there was no decisive response. Every contact hung in an unresolved suspense: no confirmation of impeding death; no assurance of his recovery. Beside the vision of hope was the specter of hopelessness. It was a time to be faith-filled; a time for every conceivable act of purification, prayer, and self-giving.

Lawrence was determined to accompany Flower and Melodie on the trip to New York in late October. It became one more way of giving himself to the Cause for which nothing must be left ungiven. When the time came, an extra suitcase packed with his medical needs, they left by train, since driving was now out of the question. Lawrence took his place with Flower on the platform, oversaw the book table, and greeted friends and guests at the lectures. It was not like all the other times, but few noticed the difference. Physically, Lawrence's face showed the strain but his smile was undimmed and about his presence emanated a depth of dedication utterly in earnest and devoid of self-consciousness. When they returned to Questhaven in early November, he opened the service that Sunday, saying, "With God, all things are possible!" His traveling to New York had seemed unthinkable, but he'd done it. And now only the deadly cancer remained.

The victory wasn't to be so swift. By mid-November he

was back in the hospital for more treatments and nearly slipped over into the inner worlds. One prayer cordon after another was called to save him. The attending doctor gave Flower no hope that he would be here through Christmas. But Lawrence made such a fight of it, even the hospital attendants had long come to marvel at the power radiating from his person and his room. In going about their duties, they found, rather than dispensing

Lawrence Newhouse around 1960

benefit, encouragement, and uplift, they were the ones receiving these kindnesses. A little cleaning woman, at a point of despair in her own life, was so transformed by a talk with Lawrence she saw her problems melt to insignificance beside the one he was surmounting.

The prayer work between the two founders never slackened and a succession of prayer cordons by the group was mounted at every recurring crisis. Lawrence had dinner with his family in a restaurant on Christmas day, a magnificent accomplishment in the face of the increasing plight within his body. Pain had not predominated over him and, when present, seemed to be mainly the side effect of cobalt treatments. What became his cross was the unending discomfort and the helpless sensation of his life force ebbing away before his loved ones and his unfinished work. He was returning to the hospital the next day for more treatments and Flower left for the mountains to spend a week in prayer, seeking renewal, and catching up on the backlog of work his illness necessitated. Late in the day she stood among the pine trees near her home looking up at a great granite dome that dominated the overhanging mountain ridge. A soft golden sheen from the setting sun fell upon everything in sight. Then, on the surface of this gigantic outcropping of stone, Lawrence's face suddenly appeared as he would look on the other side of life and she knew, for the first time, that he would soon be changing worlds. It was the loneliest, most heartbreaking moment of her life. Nothing could fill the space he would leave empty; no one could stand in his place; and though she would have her clairvoyance to occasionally contact him, the twenty-four hours of each day no more could be measured by his coming and going, its events no longer shared and placed into the perspective of a united consciousness that the conversations of a marriage alone make possible, and the irreplaceable touch of his outreaching hand, the warmth and comfort of his presence in the same room, his voice telling her how lovely she appeared in a new dress, or his eyes looking back into hers, saying what words never can say when two souls mingle as one.

January brought the final ascent of the mountain that had become Lawrence's life. The air was thin and cold; every step was labored. But his unconquerable spirit never surrendered its smile or its deathless hope. To someone who helped him become a bit more comfortable, he would look up lovingly, saying "Bless you, you are an angel of mercy."

When a friend, after a particularly difficult day, said to him, "I don't know why the best people have to suffer so," he answered, "The benefits are indescribable. God works in mysterious ways."

Towards the end, when he was admitted to the hospital for the last time, he was heard to say, "I thought I had given up all of self before, but I hadn't. Now I have given *everything, everything*. There isn't *anything* left that I haven't given over to God, even to the last breath!"

Flower was alone with him in the hospital room when he quietly crossed over into God's World. It was eleven thirty in the evening, January 29, 1963. He went like a climber disappearing into the mists near the summit of an Everest, giving with his life for the victory. Peace filled the room. He had fought the good fight. Looking at his resting face, thin and drawn by the body's tortured ordeal, Flower blinked aside tears, then said to him in the farewell of her thoughts, "Well done, thou good and faithful servant."

The dedication ceremony of the Lawrence Memorial Fountain

Chapter 18

Life without Lawrence

The day following Lawrence's transition was a new day in a new life. It seemed terribly unreal, dreamlike—as if the sun were missing from the sky with no hope of its rising again before the eyes of those who loved him and were left behind. The vacancy was permanent, obliterating even the chance of an eleventh-hour miracle; nor could anyone take his place.

For one who had lived his life without the intrusion of ego, often in the background of the mission his wife directed, and with the unassuming ease of another person journeying along the path in the company of everyone else, he now stood incredibly tall. Phone calls, telegrams, and letters came by the hundreds from as far away as Korea and Washington D.C. People Flower had never heard of stopped her on the street to tell her stories of some act of kindness or gallantry he rendered. One of the doctors who attended him throughout his siege by cancer said of Lawrence, "I have never seen anything like him. Besides being good, he was a miracle. In all my medical experience I've never observed anything like his strength, his stick-to-it-iveness, his fighting spirit. I have never had such a wonderful patient. He has left a tremendous impression upon me. He was a powerful man. About seventeen times I wrote on his chart, 'near termination' and he still lived on!"

The tributes, genuinely expressed and offered with deep feeling, told a story of the profound impact Lawrence had upon those who knew him. So unobtrusively had the strains of his life been played, blending in the pure harmony of his oneness with Flower and the Christ Cause they served, that when his music ceased, the haunting recollection of its beauty sounded in an enormous silence. Strangely, it was in this silence that his majestic power, muted by a gentleness and great-heartedness that never dominated others, now could be heard. It was a power that grew in volume with every recaptured memory of his kindly voice, every moment relived seeing again his shining face with those wonderfully bright, loving, laughing eyes. Nothing dimmed this radiance, a fact which revealed its imperial origin. It was a gift he freely gave to all the hours and everyone with the good fortune to come within his light. With it, the very atmosphere of the day was transformed by his presence. Spirits straightened, moods lifted, and thoughts quickened before the cheerful blaze of his purposefulness. Yet permeating this earnestness to serve the Lord, was a quality of eternal youth filling every activity with enthusiasm, adventure, and delight. He led others not by commands but by invitations. He won cooperation by smiles and his own exemplifying acts; never by pleading or cajoling.

Above all, he was self-giving. One of the hundreds of written tributes at his memorial service said it exactly, speaking for everyone who had ever needed his help and comfort: "Once when I was going through a difficult testing, Lawrence said: 'If you feel the need to talk to me, you come to me and no matter what I'm doing, we'll talk about your need.' Words do not express what this meant to me. It was this giving of himself which saved me from leaving Questhaven and my destiny here."

Many times Lawrence let these emergencies crowd into his tight schedule, displacing other responsibilities and delaying his arrival home where Flower waited for him to relieve her or take them on a long-awaited family outing. Where his own work was concerned, it often meant linotyping or printing until two or three in the morning to make up for the numerous interruptions. But if his giving priority to those who needed help was a fault, what a forgivable fault that was!

Flower said of Lawrence, "He possessed greatness—there was no element or trace of littleness in him. He challenged the littleness in others by his living strength and largeness of outlook." How that was Lawrence through and through. His life was unmarked by pettiness, and because of this to those who loved him he was an inspiration, and to the few who opposed his calling as a defender of the truth he cherished, an enigma.

And now he was gone. The loss to Flower was incalculable. She was still the founder and director of Questhaven Retreat, still a mother, and still a woman who felt the onrush of tears and the agony of separation each time she opened a bureau drawer or closet door to find it empty. Inside, she was still a wife and that was the tragedy: to be deeply in love with a husband beyond the wall of death and to have no hope for his return; to feel what a wife feels, and not to be able to share these feelings, nor be what a wife is and do what a wife does.

Was this the sacrifice hidden in the initiatory experience on Mt. Frazier more than three decades ago? Had she been given Lawrence as her joyous companion to prepare a place for the work and, because she had not known personal love in the last three incarnations, to prepare herself for the overcoming of grief by losing the one person with whom, in all of her lives, she had known the most fulfilling and transcendent love?

Tears were frequent in the weeks that followed, sometimes awakening little Melodie in the early hours of the morning, but despair never gained a foothold. The second Sunday after Lawrence's passing, Flower was back at the lectern, speaking again of the unbroken reality of God and the luminous inner worlds of His Realm. Her friends urged her to travel, to take a year's leave of absence, to be free of her responsibilities at Questhaven. She turned aside each suggestion appreciatively but resolutely, choosing to stand fast and face the ache inside, not letting it drive a wedge between herself and what continued to be her mission.

One change was vital. If she was to stay on alone to carry the load of channelship and motherhood, without her husband's immense assistance, another home would have to be found for Christopher with a father as firm as Lawrence had been. Her doctor measured the importance of this decision in terms of her life; he went much farther, ordering her at the same time to reduce her work load drastically. Seeing him depart, bewildered by the loss of the one person who was the center of his universe, was twice heartbreaking for Flower. What a peculiar destiny he had shared with his father, coming all the way out of the chaos of a war-ravaged country into the order of a Christian home in America. Only the sadness of his past softened the hardship of this next turn of events—that, and knowing within how much he needed discipline. Through the Holt Adoption Agency arrangements were made for Christopher to be placed in a home in another state.

One morning soon after his departure, Melodie awoke and asked, "Mother, is this all that is left of our family?"

"Yes, it is," answered Flower.

"Tragic, isn't it?" the eight-year-old replied.

❧ ✳ ☙

Together with her husband, Flower had prayed day and night for his healing to the point of complete exhaustion. After his death, it was another four months before she found the strength to pray again or to experience beauty. The interlude was without precedent in her life. From the time her Guardian took command of her spiritual training, prayer had been a daily necessity; but the great battle had drained her of the last ounce of reserve power. It then required the healing renewal that only comes with time to bring her back to the same capacity once more.

Answers now began to flow. She learned something about Lawrence she had not been allowed to know when he was alive. He had taken on this manner of death as a karmic cancellation to climax his life's endeavor. This accounted for the lack of confirmation in response to all of her previous requests for healing. For both, it had been a supreme test of faith, ending victoriously.

Telepathically she continually sensed Lawrence's presence on the higher planes of life but clairvoyantly she saw him only occasionally. He was much busier than on earth, a revelation that astonished everyone who knew him. To visibly contact him, called him away from these new and essential duties and she knew this privilege must never be exercised except in extreme emergencies. This left him free to come to her when it was permissible. At such times he shared his own impressions of life on the other side. His insights were remarkable. When she asked him how the inner worlds seemed to him, he replied that things were quite different to what he on earth had envisioned them to be. Strangely, one could not see the physical world any longer but only astral counterparts of persons, objects, and places. He could only see Flower in her higher bodies, and these were quite different than his memory of her physical form.

At first he was filled with homesickness for his family and work but this feeling was dispelled as teachers showed him how to help without remaining so close to them. He related that for several weeks he was visited by relatives and friends who had learned of his return. He also had begun attending sessions in the Halls of Learning where he heard both the Masters he already knew, and Adepts unfamiliar to him.

He told his beloved that as long as his family grieved for him he was instructed to remain near them so they could sense his presence. As their longing quieted, he was able to venture greater distances from them, keeping in close attunement telepathically. He then delighted in visiting great mountains and deva temples to exult in the flashing color streams and the music tones radiating from these strongholds.

What he deeply regretted, he said, was the time he had wasted on earth. Nothing could have struck those with whom Flower shared this observation more forcibly: of all people, Lawrence possessed a boundless energy that seemed never to rest. He was forever busy, always about a duty or a kindness, even if it was to welcome a visitor to the Retreat or give a word of encouragement to a brother or sister undergoing a trial. Flower explained this paradox as a valuable lesson in the relative degree of awakeness between our world and his. Lawrence now lived in realms of pure consciousness where sleep was no longer necessary. Every moment seethed with undreamed-of potentialities. Discovering this amazing contrast between what he achieved in the earth dimension and what is actually possible when every barrier of human preoccupation is dissolved, led him to this most unexpected of confessions.

On another occasion he showed her plans of a lovely studio home he was preparing for them, explaining it was as difficult to create finished and perfect houses in the heaven worlds as to erect them on earth. "This is where training in meditation helps," he told her, "as you learn to see things clearly and to manifest them truly according to design. Some persons in the astral world live in homes that are poorly constructed simply because they lack persistence and the know-how to think things into manifestation properly."

Speaking about the unhurried way one could think along certain lines, Lawrence said, "Here all one's thinking is straightened out and corrected, but it requires earth to prove one has benefited and changed."

Once, while on a walk in nature, Flower felt the desire to see him but didn't wish to disturb him. Instantly she saw him studying an Akashic Record's account of a Grecian tableau used in initiatory rites. She watched him from an angle off to one side until she felt content. Then, in the mountains, he came to her and told of the highest event yet realized: to have heard the Lord Christ speaking to a multitude of gathered souls; and those who had most recently arrived in the inner dimension were seated closest to the Lord. Lawrence's face shone as he related what the talk had meant to him. He said no artist on earth could do justice to a picture of the Christ as he is.

July eighteenth of the year of Lawrence's passing was a particularly hard day for Flower; it was his birthday—a day in every other year of their marriage given to the happiest of activities: a long walk in the mountains, dinner at a favorite restaurant, and perhaps visiting an art gallery. All day she struggled to rise above her feelings, yet honor him in everything she did. Towards evening, he came to her and said, "Now you are to live in touch with me by faith—by developing a new branch of faith which will encourage and make possible our communion."

The great comfort of this message caused her to turn to a file in which he had kept notations of inner experiences while on earth. Her eyes fell upon a record in his own handwriting of a dream he'd had in 1952 which, she remembered telling him at the time, had been an actual contact with a Master on the inner planes. As she read through its account, she realized it closely resembled the kind of events he now was undergoing:

"A dream unfolded regarding a musical concert at which Flower and I were speaking between numbers. At the close of it, I felt myself being lifted up and drawn swiftly through the upper atmosphere. As I passed over great forests and meadows, I perceived occasionally, down below me on the ground, large giant figures, each enveloped in a gigantic aura of Light. Perhaps these were advanced nature beings in charge of younger nature lives.

"Up and up I was drawn by a beneficent force which was responsible for my flight through space. Very soon I was brought to a standstill, poised in the air and scintillating with a spiritual quickening which was akin to the highest spiritual inspiration I had ever felt—only stronger.

"I then observed the noble, strong and handsome young figure of an advanced initiate who seemed very familiar—like a dearly loved elder Brother whom I had not seen for a long time but whose countenance had been deeply impressed upon my memory. He moved around me in a circular way, turning me as he did so, and took his place beside me on my left. I knew he was in complete control of my placement. It was a good feeling—as though I was in very good care. I felt no fear—only awe and wonder at the mysterious events which were taking place. His body was slender and tall, and the outstanding impressions were that he glowed from within with a soft gold light, and his radiance sent forth a strong emanation of love and joyousness. A wave of admiration and devotion swept forth from my soul to him.

"In this poised position I felt and saw the envelopment of Light which was radiant everywhere. Every particle of the atmosphere glowed with a soft white Light.

"My attention was next directed to a ceremony already in progress. Two high initiates or Masters—a man and a woman—were praying and making religious ceremonial motions beside and above an altar-like structure. The top of this circular altar appeared to be a living human head, facing upward. From the mouth of this beneficent face came a flowing stream of opaque Light which rose with a fountain-like movement and then radiated its vibrant energies to us and to everything

204

in the area round about. The fountain-like stream of energy seemed to descend to great distances far below where we stood, presumably being directed earthward for the blessing of the world.

"Not very distinguishable, but most strongly felt, was the presence of a great Lord who also glowed from within with a rich golden light. Every atom of his being seemed to be sending forth an emanation of Light. This glorious figure likewise performed a symbolic ritual, speaking in a tongue I could not understand. Yet the power I sensed coming from him was most wonderful.

"The picture changed gradually and I beheld this large lordly figure on three levels at the same time. I saw three identical figures with a level floor or platform separating them from each other. On each level the figure was engaged in identical actions simultaneously. There were slight variations in color and scenery on the three levels.

"As the experience closed I felt myself descending to a lower sphere. As I glided downward, every atom of my being tingled with the power of the experience. I was reluctant to return and paused at a "boundary" where I sought intently to retain the memory of the preceding happenings. Several times, as I wavered at the crossing of the boundary, I found that I was failing to carry through the full memory of details. Returning to the other side, I made new attempts to refresh my memory and reimpress my mind, resolutely determined to retain more and more of the details. Finally I reluctantly returned, content to bring what fragments I could remember into awakened, physical consciousness.

"As I came to partial wakefulness, I loitered as long as possible in this state, to enjoy to the full the inspiring, thrilling, tingling, upliftment which vibrated throughout my whole being—even the physical body.

"The next day, I felt hopeful that the great escort who had

been responsible for my journey into Light was the Master John. This was confirmed in instruction from him through Flower: 'Yes, my pupil Lawrence, I was with you and you with me last evening The larger figure was your insight into one aspect of the Ancient of Days.' "

Six months, then nearly a year passed since his return to the eternal Homeland. Flower quietly, inconspicuously overcame the hurt his loss had inflicted. She kept up her lecturing schedule on Sundays at Questhaven and the writing of a new series of monthly instructions called the Quest lessons. These soon emerged as the quintessence of her teachings: a synthesis of new information interspersed with restatements of many of her earlier writings. Interviews were no longer scheduled and only occurred when she felt strongly led to speak to a particular individual who was at a point of unusual spiritual readiness.

At every opportunity, though scarcely often enough, she slipped away to her home in Idyllwild. "The mountains are my oxygen," she reflected. "If people knew how my soul holds its breath for these occasions, they would understand why this recharging is so essential to me." She described one of its peaks as an initiatory mountain overlooked by a magnificent nature lord. His power at once tested and rekindled each person coming into the auric mantle of his particular mountain stronghold. Gradually, the upsurging, healing emanations of light unique to this nature temple gave back her strength and with it the grasp of beauty and receptivity to the inner worlds she had steadfastly known.

Christmas Eve of 1963, only eleven months after Lawrence's transition, she joined a number of the Questhaven group in the Chapel of the Holy Quest to prepare, as she traditionally had done at other Christmastides, for the year's highest experience—the Christ Procession at midnight. For nearly an hour they sang carols together. Then at 11:30 the overhead lights were turned out, leaving the gathering silently meditating before the altar aglow with soft candle light.

Flower asked them to empty their hearts of every burden to make space for the entrance of the Lord Christ. "We have come to worship the Holy One," she said. "As we meditate, let our minds and emotions be purified."

After a pause, she explained how prior to the midnight hour there is much Angelic activity. "Wherever people gather in worship at this hour, great Angels in vast numbers attend them. They increase the blue, rose and lavender hues in the atmosphere which have accumulated with Angelic and human devotions since Thanksgiving. Our prayers resemble clouds of colorful and fragrant incense that rise from us and travel upward toward the higher worlds."

Another period of silence passed, then between brief pauses she began describing the entire extraordinary scene as one might narrate the growing splendor of a glorious sunrise. "Brightness is already forming all around this time zone of the earth. Music is now faintly audible to me. As the music swells, an active movement of vibrating symbols revolves in the spaces confronting us. The symbols 'V' and 'M' are frequently discernible. Both of these letters are in white.

The music is stronger now. It is made up of thousands of voices singing in tones rather than words.

The atmosphere is growing more blue, the madonna blue shade. And way behind us in the west, the air has caught the colors that are broadcast from the east. The Angelic hosts who are present reflect the glory of the aerial colors and their voices join the choirs of the oncoming singers."

Except for Flower's voice advancing with each new glimpse of inner revelation, the chapel seemed suspended in a great stillness intensified by the expectation each listener now felt. Flower continued. "Just as immense clouds can partly hide the sunrise in the morning, the billowing forma-

207

tions of color veil some of the glory Light that is beginning to pierce the east. A great stream of silver rays shines out before the Christ Presence. They represent the quickening power. Shining from within the colorful clouds of concealment are occasional streams of fiery gold. When the Christ appears the clouds will vanish and the golden Light will blaze forth upon the world. The Christ will descend into the lowest level of the etheric plane, as he does in this ceremonial way every Christmas Eve.

"Large white circles of billowing essences are disengaged from huge cloud formations—and they circulate throughout the atmosphere dispensing their powers. Whatever they touch feels the contact."

Another pause, then: "There are sounds like blaring trumpets now, coming from the east, and the light is growing quite intense."

Silence again. "When I say, 'The Lord is come,' he will be passing at that moment. That will be the time to proffer him your inner gift . . . Very high Angel Awakeners and Angel Princes are opening the Path. The white clouds have disappeared and in their stead is a tremendous brilliance of blending color.

"Now, golden emanations are beginning to move through our part of the world, right here through our chapel.

"The Lord is come, let earth receive her King. The Lord Emmanuel stands majestically tall and calm. He is in a white robe. His resounding words are 'Behold. Be awake, and your life shall be reclaimed.'

"Behind the Lord Christ is the renowned Sanat Kumara, the Lord of the World. He is an ancient Initiate. Directly behind the Sanat Kumara are the Lord Maha Chohan and the Lord Buddha. Then follow the eminent elder brothers and sisters, in deep meditation and in rows of twelve. There are eight lines of Adepts.

"Now the initiates are visible, also in rows of twelve. Lawrence is among them. As he passed, a beautiful golden-orbed thought form fell into our chapel. The body of initiates is so lengthy, they are still visible. None of these figures are actually moving. They are standing still. It is the movement of the planet which causes them to appear to advance.

"Now is visible that endless body of consecrated souls who form the strong backbone of our humanity. Most of them are in white vestments. The initiates were robed in many colors.

"With the Lord Christ's passing came a golden burst of Light and then golden flecks appeared to be falling like snow onto the earth. As they fell they assumed geometrical patterns. Should any aura be touched by one of these flecks it will be charged with a Christ idea.

"The band of dedicated souls is singing with the hosts of Angels that rise tier above tier over the human beings in the procession.

"The whole inner world appears opened and it is easy to observe—to note the colorful landscape behind the figures.

There are tall, tremendous mountains composed of something like a crystalline nature. From these mountains flashes shine out.

"The Christ's nativity procession has not ended, but the most exalted Ones have moved beyond our range of vision. It is well for us to disband and retire as soon as possible so that we too, in our inner bodies, may join the throngs who are praising Christ."

That night, as each of the group silently turned homeward, what they had heard and sensed, and in part seen, mingled together in a rare chemistry of mysticism. How commonplace all the other Christmases now seemed, before their spending such a Christmas Eve with Flower. Her eyes were like a marvelous telescope that could penetrate past the cloud layers blinding earth to the surrounding heavens and bring the stars seemingly near enough to hold in one's hands.

Chapter 19

Travel and the Start of a Tax Battle

Learning to live without Lawrence's companionship and practical talents brought Flower to new thresholds of independence and inner strength. But what still pulled at her from behind like a great stone dragging from a chain, was her health. There were both good and bad days, fluctuating with the pressures of work, the demands of people, delays in getting to the mountains, and the ability of the supporting staff at Questhaven to sense her needs. It was now necessary to have checkups on her heart activity every two or three months. Yet even with the uncertainty of how she would feel from day to day she seldom altered her schedule of commitments. There were many Sunday mornings when she would arrive at the Chapel too nauseous or faint to stand for more than a minute or two, but by ten forty-five when the carillon bells announced the beginning of worship she would be ready without an outer sign of hesitancy.

During the next several years her Guardian instructed her to travel extensively. In April of 1964 she accepted a lecture invitation in London. Knowing that one of her purposes was to gain impressions clairvoyantly of European countries, she was alert to the auric radiations describing each place on her itinerary.

She arrived in England to find spring in full flower. The inner colors of Britain she found to be a mixture of yellow, light green and apricot. Italy, her next stop, proved to be a coral shade interwoven with areas of bright red. She loved the fountains of Rome and the Roman ruins, except for the

Coliseum with its heavy residue of tragedy. St. Peter's was also a highlight spiritually and the seat of a most powerful first ray beam; but the place that impressed her most was the Chapel of the Holy Spirit off to one side of this magnificent cathedral. The currents of love and compassion that filled this small chapel were so strong that it brought a torrent of tears to her eyes. Reinforcing this reaction was the sight of a great Angel adoringly focusing his light on every worshiper.

While driving with friends from Rome to Florence, they stopped for several hours at Assisi. What a thrilling scene to behold inwardly! Miles from the hilltop village where St. Francis lived and served, she saw a huge archetype which resembled a flashing clear blue jewel whose center contained a translucent white cross. As they approached Assisi she realized this symbol formed the center of a blue beam that poured into the Basilica where St. Francis was buried.

Florence was a gem of spiritual qualities. There was more coral present in the aura of the place and less red than she had observed elsewhere in Italy. As the birthplace of the renaissance, its superphysical energies were unusually active, flowing through its churches, palaces, galleries, and breathtaking gardens. The beam serving this city was of the fourth ray, creating an etheric superstructure of indescribable beauty. About the monastery where Fra Angelico lived and painted was an enfoldment of glowing peach-colored light. Never had she seen so many Adepts of this artistic ray in one location before.

Next, she visited Switzerland. Its unearthly grandeur caught Flower unprepared, scarcely believing what her physical senses reported. Then, in the area about Interlaken, she realized the etheric plane blended so imperceptibly with its outer counterpart that one saw here what is active in the etheric world. This, too, was a new experience.

Switzerland's aura was peach with an occasional contrasting tone of deep green. A personal triumph came when she took the narrow gauge railroad to an 11,333 foot plateau just below the Jungfrau. Here and elsewhere throughout Switzerland, Austria and Germany, the beings she observed about the mountains were colossal in height and radiated energies of tremendous magnitude.

The gentleness of Switzerland's mountains gave way to dynamic power presences as she entered Austria. Innsbruck, Salzburg, and Vienna shared auras combining shades of green and deep blue.

In Germany, Flower visited Oberammergau, another city overshadowed by a gleaming archetype symbolizing its steadfast performance of the Passion Play every ten years honoring a pledge given in 1633 when the city was saved from the plague.

A year later, again in April, Flower was directed to travel to Mexico. She was told by this high initiate there was a special place she must see and that further revelation would be given when that site was reached. This time she was allowed to take twelve persons with her, including Melodie and Galen. It would not be a pleasure trip, but a spiritual journey to discover the inner nature of this neighboring country. It formed the model upon which were based all subsequent tours Flower later would lead.

Two rules were given the group as they prepared to depart from the airport in Tijuana for Guadalajara, Mexico: to practice cheerfulness and unselfishness throughout the trip. Then each evening when possible the group would meet to share the golden moments of that day.

As they passed from Guadalajara to Lake Chapala to San Miguel de Allende, Flower wondered whether one of these places would prove to be the promised site. Then, driving into Patzcuaro on the way to Mexico City, she noticed a striking difference in the atmosphere. While in the simple charm of this village the initiate again came to her and announced that this was the chosen center to which they'd been led. Here, over the waters of beautiful Lake Patzcuaro, was one of the earth's great power centers—a planetary chakra. Super-physically, it was visible as a large archetype shining above the Indian village of Janitzio on an island in the lake. In this dazzling archetype shone seven jewel-like symbols represent-ing the seven rays.

Later, in Mexico City, two inner experiences occurred which greatly impressed Flower. The first came to Lawrence's mother who had never had a conscious encounter with a visi-tor from the inner worlds before. She was awakened in the night to find in her room a man of great dignity, clothed in priestly Indian raiment. His arms were outstretched toward the windows. She called out to the other woman sharing her room but couldn't arouse her. While she watched this figure, he slowly walked out of the room and into the night air.

The second experience grew out of the first, as it became apparent later. Flower observed this same initiate going to ev-ery sleeping person, summoning them into the astral planes to accompany him to the inner temple poised at the summit of Mount Popocatepetl. She recalled looking back to see if the others were on their way. Cautiously, they came, one by one. Ahead gleamed the temple. It shone as if the alabaster-like material were incandescent. The building was tall and circu-lar in shape. It contained twelve open doors through which their group with others strange to Flower passed. Above the entrances and seated on a great dais was a figure clad in gold cloth. This man was unusually large and everyone was led to stand before him where he was meditating. Flower now real-ized that he was the Lord or Guardian Spirit of this mountain. In the center of the bare white gleaming temple was a flaming spire as high as the edifice itself. This fiery column Flower observed to be at least three feet wide and its curling swirls contained colors both of earth and some she'd seen only in higher states of consciousness. At the base of this mysterious fire which emanated no heat, but rather a pleasant cool sensation, was a square white plaque in which hieroglyphics were engraved. As she studied them their meaning gradually became clear. They said: "All who enter herein will be free from limitation and imperfection."

Some of the group, including Flower, tried to enter the fire but a strange foreboding stopped each of them. Then she realized that if she, or any of the others,

Flower sharing on a trip to Mt. Frazier

entered the fire it would precipitate transition. Looking at her children she realized this meant she would no longer be with them, and her love for them and their need made her step aside.

When Flower shared these happenings with the group the next evening, they listened with intense interest. It was then that Lawrence's mother was prompted to share her own encounter.

❧ ✳ ❧

Moments of luminosity spent with Flower such as these formed deep impressions in those who found the way clear to share them. But wherever Flower was, whether traveling, in the mountains, or at Questhaven, such moments were always possible. Mostly, they occurred in nature, including all of her life's highest illuminations. And what was usual for her on any day in the week would have struck the average seeker as a once-in-a-lifetime revelation, like the Music of the Spheres. At certain times throughout the year these became audible to her. Always during the summer she made it a point to go outdoors before retiring. She then focused her eyes on the canopy of silvery stars for several minutes, when all in her was at *full attention*. Then, gradually, the music was faintly heard and as the seconds passed the volume increased until wave upon wave of harmonious melody swept through the Retreat. As the more gentle strains moved beyond her hearing, other notes, stronger, more stirring and victorious, sounded across the skies. Later, on the crisp nights of fall and winter, the music possessed still greater strength and grandeur. Only reluctantly, on any such evening, did she take leave of this wonder returning to her bedroom with the quiet realization that, with sleep, she would again join these soulic strains, and greater marvels still. Sleep, for Flower, meant freedom to return again into the temples and holy grounds of the inner worlds. While her outer vehicle rested, her inner bodies soared to vantage points chosen by her Guardian.

One morning, while meditating in the chapel for the well-being and protection of Questhaven—a vigil she kept daily—the unresolved problem of the Retreat's tax exempt status came vividly to her attention. For most of the years Lawrence was with her, the county assessor had granted only one of its six hundred and forty acres as necessary for the fulfillment of its religious purpose. Lawrence wrote letter after letter of protest, visited the assessor's office, and finally gained the concession of a few additional acres based on the new chapel, its parking lot, and other improvements. All the while, Questhaven's greatest spiritual assets—more than six hundred outlying acres of secluded hills luxuriantly clothed in chaparral and shady canyons strewn with groves of live oaks—were judged superfluous.

The answer came to her, swiftly and clearly: if the tax assessor refused to see the religious use of every acre within the Retreat's boundaries, the matter must be decided by a court. A call was made to their lawyer and legal proceedings began. When Questhaven's tax bill for the new fiscal year arrived, the practical merit of Flower's intuition was validated—it had nearly tripled. Though every acre had been purchased to create a nature retreat, a protected ring of hills filled with native beauty to inspire the worshiper, at the current rate of the increasing property tax, within ten years Questhaven could be paying as much as one hundred thousand dollars annually. Yet every acre was used exclusively for drawing closer to God, and, in the legal language of the Ministry's incorporation papers, "irrevocably dedicated in perpetuity" to this purpose.

In January of 1967 the case went to court. Once more at stake, though not the issue on which the lawsuit hinged, was Questhaven's survival in the years to come. The loss of this case would surely close the door to any future change of viewpoint by the assessor. It would mean the difference between a Questhaven of its present optimum size or one restricted to the existing central area, described by the assessor as thirty-one acres. The law firm handling the case had not urged legal action, foreseeing the risk of getting nothing and being unable to work out additional concessions in the years ahead. But for Flower only one point mattered: the land was obtained for religious purposes, and would always be used for religious purposes. Her conception of the case was courageously simple: "When you are in the right, and this right is not recognized, you must fight for that right, all the way, with everything you have to give!"

The battle proceeded. In the opening arguments, the issue before the court was precisely pinpointed: the tax exemption code of California granted property tax exemption for "religious use." The assessor's office arbitrarily interpreted this to mean *physical use for a religious purpose*: if, to this end, one placed buildings on the land, put in roads, parking lots, walkways, and reasonable landscaping—then one was using the land.

To exempt even a single acre of unimproved land that lacked physical use was quite unthinkable. The position of Questhaven was in direct opposition: when land, untouched by the hand of man, was used to create an aesthetic and inspirational setting in which to foster the experience of God in nature, that, too, was religious use.

Witnesses testified, facts were entered into evidence, and points of law were argued back and forth. The county counsel went so far as to exclude all of Questhaven's supporters from the courtroom. Unlike the earlier trial against the trespasser which, thanks to Lawrence's exhaustive collection of evidence, never appeared in jeopardy, the outcome of this case hung on the delicate balance of what was meant by the two words, "religious use." Surprisingly, the judge chose not to visit the grounds to see them for himself. When final arguments were given on the fifth day, the Questhaven lawyer concluded with the eloquent and moving analogy that, given the logic of the assessor's office, only the rock on which Christ prayed in the Garden of Gethsemane would have been exempted. Then the judge closed his book of notes, thanked everyone, and said his decision would be handed down within sixty days.

There was nothing to do but wait—and pray. The trial had gone as well as the lawyers had expected. The right facts were before the court, every useful argument had been offered, and now the judge would have to spell out the meaning of the two vital words, thus deciding the case. There was another uncomfortable possibility: he could decide in Questhaven's favor but still exempt only a small portion of the six hundred and forty acres—whatever he felt was sufficient for the activities described to him. When the lawyers were asked to speculate on the outcome, one of them shrugged his shoulders and said simply, "Every lawsuit has a winner and a loser—don't ask me what goes on in a judge's mind." Then he thought a moment and added, "I never like to be a loser."

Weeks passed and no word from the court. The ardent prayer work continued and the suspense grew. "Why was it taking so long?" Flower wondered. Finally, as the sixty day period came to an end, the verdict ar-

Flower A. Newhouse around 1970

rived in the law firm's mail. A phone call brought the fateful decision: Questhaven had lost the case. The judge sided completely with the county on every point. Nothing had been gained and the future was more ominous than ever.

The following Sunday, as she stood in the narthex of the chapel waiting to process to the altar behind the choir, she turned to her assistant and said: "I think we should appeal this case right up to the supreme court, if need be." She still stood by her rule for the right: "You must fight, all the way, with everything you have!"

The next day when the law firm was advised of this decision, they balked. Appealing a case, the senior lawyer of the firm explained is to go against the odds. He pointed out that the court system was so constructed as to uphold, not reverse, lower court rulings; otherwise, the law would be in a constant state of flux, never offering a firm foothold. The wiser reaction, he counseled, would be to extend the physical use of Questhaven with more buildings, more roads, and more landscaping and gain whatever additional acres the assessor might grant. His last argument was even more realistic: to continue the case to higher courts would be quite expensive.

Flower shook her head decisively when the lawyer's advice was explained to her. "We would be destroying everything we purchased Questhaven for—its natural beauty. We also would be giving in to the very forces that oppose us," she responded. But her final argument struck home with the greatest force: "These are the Lord's acres—we cannot fail him or the work that he has given for us to establish."

Before overruling the Retreat's own attorneys, an opinion by a second law firm specializing in tax litigation was obtained. Its recommendation in favor of filing an appeal delighted Flower, making the point that the lower court judge had arbitrarily narrowed the interpretation of the tax exemption code, offering an appeals court a clear opening to disagree with him.

The motion for an appeal was prepared and filed. It would be a slow, methodical process—about two years. But once more there was hope.

Chapter 20

Adventures, Conquest and Enlightenment

That fall, Flower led thirty-four people on a month-long tour of South America. Its purposes were to observe the spiritual emanations of this continent as they moved from country to country and to become acquainted with the people and culture of each. Chile, along the southern range of the Andes on the Pacific side, was destined in another five hundred years to become the next cradle of a new race. There were also the remains of Incan and Pre-Incan civilizations to revisit, since at one time or another each of the group had lived in this land.

After spending several days in Rio de Janeiro, the most imposing city of the trip, they left for Buenos Aires, arriving in the midst of torrential rains. They accomplished what sightseeing was possible and prepared to depart, this time for the exquisite lake country straddling the border between Argentina and Chile where everyone looked forward to its breathtaking scenery and a change in the weather.

Reaching the airport early the next morning, they found it badly flooded and most of the schedules canceled. Hours dragged by and finally there was room in one flight for seven of the party. The rest had to wait until the following day, with no change in the rain-drenched conditions. When an aircraft finally was available they climbed on board, thankful that at last they would be off for the bejeweled lakes of Bariloche. Suddenly an ominous feeling filled the crowded cabin. The captain had passed down the aisle toward the cockpit visibly upset, apparently angered at being ordered to fly in such foul weather. Flower, detecting the danger of his mood, attempted to gather her group together and disembark from the plane but the captain refused permission and started the engines. Then, jerking the propeller-driven aircraft around, he gunned it down the taxi runway in a wild bouncing dash to the take-off apron. Flower glanced out the window and a chill swept through her whole being: off to one side she saw several Angels of Death waiting alertly; Lawrence was with them. Something terrible was about to happen. Just then the pilot, having overshot the apron, slammed on the wheel brakes and the plane skidded out of control, plunging off the concrete runway. As the wheel on the port side sank into the mud, it collapsed, forcing the wing to plunge downward, driving the engines into the ground. Instantly, one of the propellers tore loose from its shaft and slashed through the cabin, missing her son Galen by inches. Mercifully, nothing caught fire and the ill-fated craft came to a lurching halt.

The captain soon emerged from the cockpit, shaken and humbled. "Forgive what has happened," he begged. "This is the darkest day of my life." Somehow his words sounded strangely beautiful to Flower. They were, after all, alive and unhurt. She looked out her window again and the great Angels, along with Lawrence, had departed. Gratitude flooded over her—first, for the safety of her party but second, for the instancy of enfoldment those on the inner side of life stand ready to give in emergencies.

Bariloche was everything they wished it to be: majestic grandeur and pristine beauty, along with warm-hearted people and delightful accommodations. After the earthy extravagance of Rio and the drama of Buenos Aires, the journey now opened out onto its enchanting exploration of South America's west coast. Chile won them completely with its fondness for North Americans and its endearing courtesies. Cuzco and the storied lost city of Macchu Picchu in Peru thrilled everyone and the sight of Incan splendor stirred many sleeping memories. On a peak opposite the deserted fortress of the latter stands a spectacular site where the Master of South America has his residence on the inner planes.

Then came incomparable Bogota, Colombia, set like a gem into a mountain fastness, color-rich Guatemala with boundless hospitality and charm, and finally, Mexico—gay, romantic and picturesque—an everlasting favorite.

The return to Questhaven was a bright homecoming—how close it had come that most of her party might never have seen it again. Every hill, every tree, every cottage seemed to embrace them in reunion. Even before she had finished unpacking, Flower was filling the bird feeders and bird baths, setting out tidbits for the other wildlings, and lavishing love upon her many dogs and cats. How good it was to be home!

Then in the fall the Masters returned, instructing Flower that they were beginning a fresh series of lessons. For many, never having shared in this unique instruction, it came as a never-to-be-forgotten experience; but few ever realized the exhausting discipline of alignment it demanded of her. Somehow, whatever Flower did always seemed to come effortlessly. It never occurred to most people that Flower often struggled to bring herself to the uncompromising threshold necessitated for direct channelship with a Master. And, in fact, she never outwardly evidenced the struggle when it was taking place. She once described what it was like to receive the words of an Adept. Sometimes they came to her clearly and easily, as in a moment of great inspiration, only far more concrete and reliable. Their thoughts would take a form resembling "spinning tops," releasing their archetypal impressions like colorful and marvelously fashioned hieroglyphics, triggering her recognition and enabling her to express precisely their equivalence in her own words. Occasionally, if she was tired or distracted by latecomers to the chapel, they appeared hazy and indistinct, rushing at her profusely. When this happened, the Master would end the instruction until a more favorable time.

These latest lessons brimmed with rich insights into the challenges of discipleship. A new Master, under whom many had studied centuries earlier in Italy, was a specialist in para-psychology and shared invaluable teachings on the nature of spiritual impressions and creative receptivity. Of the many messages that were given in the next few months, one from the Master who first came in August of 1950, more than seventeen years earlier, revealed glimpses of Questhaven's own purpose: "Years ago it was decided that this place should be set apart for a Work sponsored by hierarchical officiants. We chose Questhaven because of its geographical location and its spiritual qualities of magnetism. Later, we saw to it that Flower and Lawrence were guided to Questhaven, and we helped to call each of you from distant places that you might be a part of this cluster under the direction of the Inner Government of the World. We have several such groups throughout the planet, each one unique and specialized. The particular work that is aimed at here is one whose roots and trunk of the Tree of Expression is that of Christian mysticism. There is no other group with exactly this emphasis."

About the middle of December, on one of these matchless days of instruction, a most extraordinary thing happened. Southern California received a rare snowfall. Questhaven itself, never having experienced snow in the memory of the area's oldest inhabitants, looked like a Christmas fairyland with nearly six inches of snow covering everything in sight. It seemed to say, "Surprise—all things are possible for those who believe!"

If that was its omen, the forecast was soon to be startlingly fulfilled. A few days after Easter, 1969, an excited phone call came from Questhaven's lawyer. In the morning's mail had come the appellate court's decision in review of the tax exemption case. The verdict: a unanimous reversal of the lower court's ruling. "This is an amazing victory," he emphasized. "You really are to be congratulated for standing by your convictions, especially in the face of our pessimism."

The opinion handed down by four judges read in part: "In finding the shrines, meditation and rest sites, and the trails connecting them with the central area were the only areas used by retreatants the court confined their purpose in using them to walking, sitting or standing. Eliminated from consideration was the environment in which the retreatants walked, sat or stood, which was furnished by the surrounding property maintained in its natural state. It would be absurd to hold the only part of the property within the boundaries of a national park used by visitors for park purposes is that improved with roads and trails. It is equally absurd to hold the only part of the property within the boundaries of a site maintained to provide an atmosphere conducive to prayer, meditation and contemplation used by retreatants for this purpose is that improved with trails, shrines, meditation and rest sites.... In determining whether the amount of property reasonably necessary to provide a site for retreatants conducive to prayer, meditation and contemplation in the manner provided at Questhaven, the determination of those responsible for carrying out the religious purposes of the Christward Ministry should be respected."

"This is a most unusual ruling," the lawyer exclaimed. "Decisions like this only come along once in a great while. They make new law for the entire state and what you have achieved sets into motion a whole new outlook for setting aside undeveloped land to remain as a natural sanctuary for future generations."

Such a ruling, however, did not automatically grant the Retreat with its tax exemption. Instead, it sent the case back to the Superior Court for retrial, given the Appellate Court's unanimous ruling.

To spare the Retreat the expense of a second trial, their attorney filed a motion for summary judgment—a legal maneuver whereby one side in a retrial situation claims that the evidence on record from the first trial, along with the successful appellate ruling, is sufficient to decide the case in their favor, without further litigation. The motion was filed and in due course a court hearing was scheduled before a Judge Hugo Fisher. On the day of the hearing Judge Fisher opened his remarks with a surprising announcement. Noting that Questhaven Retreat was a Christian center, he chose to inform its attorney that he was himself Jewish, an atheist, and a member of the Unitarian Church. As such, he was opposed on principle to the tax exemption of religious property. Having said that, he asked the Retreat's attorney if he still wished to pursue a summary judgment in his court? Questhaven's attorney thanked the court for its candor and withdrew the motion. As he left the courtroom, he said to the Retreat's representatives, "That was a close one." Clearly, Judge Fisher was sending a message of where he would be coming from in reviewing the evidence.

This meant another full retrial of the case now had to be conducted. Several weeks passed and finally the time came for courtroom assignment. Because the assignment of a judge was such an important factor in the outcome of a trial, Questhaven's attorney prepared two lists of the available judges— a list of those who were inclined to favor the county, based on their prior courtroom decisions, and another of those inclined to be neutral or not to favor the county. This was important since each party in a lawsuit has the right of one challenge, allowing them to reject the assignment of one judge if they feel that one is not likely to favor their client.

When the Ministry's case was announced, the next courtroom available belonged to the one judge most prone to rule against them. Without hesitation, the Retreat's attorney challenged him. The assignment clerk then selected the next available courtroom, and unbelievably, it belonged to Judge Fisher! Stunned, the attorney appealed for reconsideration, but none was allowed. As if fortune had cruelly turned against the Retreat, a small gathering of Questhaven's faithful pondered the meaning of this strange twist of fate. After the near-miraculous turnaround with the Appellate Court victory, how could this now be in jeopardy?

As the second trial began, however, quite the opposite emerged. Judge Fisher, it turned out, was one of the judges the County attorney had planned to challenge because of his unpredictable courtroom record. Seeing Questhaven's attorney being dismayed at this turn of events, he decided to go along with Judge Fisher. One of the first things the Judge did was to schedule a visit to Questhaven Retreat. When that day came, he was obviously pleased to find it so natural and pristine. It was then learned that Judge Fisher previously had been the director of forestry for the State of California, and as a judge with an enlightened view of the environment, Questhaven could not have chosen a more sympathetic courtroom.

There was a problem, however. Judge Fisher was temperamental in how he conducted his court and often became irritated by one side or the other in how they proceeded with their respective cases. As the trial came down to final arguments, the Judge became particularly impatient with Questhaven's attorney. Stephen Isaac, who was working with the attorneys on behalf of the ministry, sensed that the Judge was looking for something missing that was vital to their case. The night before the summation arguments were due, Stephen was searching through his notes to uncover whatever might have been omitted. Retiring for the night, he tossed and turned, unable to shake himself free of the impression that a key argument or piece of evidence had been overlooked.

Then, in the early morning hours, half awake, he had a vision. In the center of this scene was the Retreat's principal display, a three dimensional model realistically recreating Questhaven's 640 acres, including its many miles of trails. But the trail system, instead of its original pathways of yellow lines branching throughout the property, now had come alive and were like pulsating bright red arteries boldly signaling their presence. In a flash, it came to the director that the Retreat's trail system held the key to their entire case. The county attorney, in making his arguments to the court in the original trial, claimed that physical use was a prerequisite to gaining tax exemption. In so doing the county was conceding that the Retreat's trails met this standard of physical use and added an additional nine acres of exempt property based on a calculation of a trail system three feet wide times twenty miles in length. Since the county was willing to exempt the tread of the Retreat's trails, and these trails permeated the Retreat's property, this fact combined with the Appellate Court's analogy to Yosemite National Park and its highway system, made the landscape surrounding the trails the real property worthy of exemption.

The following day, Stephen insisted that their attorney make this point in the final arguments. He agreed although he felt this fact was self-evident and unnecessary. When he presented this to Judge Fisher, he exploded in frustration, accusing the attorney of holding back on the case's essential argument to the very end. After hearing the remainder of the final arguments, he surprised everyone by rendering his decision directly from the bench, awarding Questhaven Retreat the tax exemption of all but fourteen acres of its 640 acre property.

It was a magnificent victory, and one allowing the Retreat to take a deep sigh of relief. Flower herself, who had taken the stand as a witness during this second trial to defend her life work, was in Japan on a world tour, when she got the call announcing the verdict. It was a joyous piece of news for her and the group accompanying her, and cause for both celebration and thanksgiving.

What happened next in this unfolding drama of the Retreat's tax exemption couldn't have been more cynical. When the new tax bills were received, there was no recognition of the court victory. The tax assessor billed the Retreat as if nothing had ever been litigated. They were back to their original tax levy prior to their court action. Believing at first that it was a bureaucratic mixup, their attorney was immediately contacted to correct the oversight. When he called back, the news was unbelievable. The county tax assessor, under the advisement of the county counsel who handled the second trial, had refunded taxes for the three year period officially litigated. Then, having the authority to determine anew the current tax levy, he now took the position that the Retreat, except for the three years litigated, was back to its original pretrial nonexempt status.

It was an unthinkable position for the county to take, and one that required the Retreat to endure a third full trial in the Superior Courts to settle the matter. When the third judge heard the case through its entirety, he not only ruled that the Retreat's acreage was completely exempt from taxation, but that he never wanted to see this case in court ever again.

Curiously, the belligerent county attorney, Mr. K, two years later turned to politics and was elected to the California State Assembly. The Retreat's reaction, at first, was one of relief that he was no longer in the county to cause further trouble. Then came a most unsettling phone call from one of the senior partners in the Retreat's law firm. He had noticed an item in his morning's newspaper that Assemblyman K was sponsoring a bill in the state legislature that imposed limits on the amount of land that could be tax exempt for religious use. An immediate phone call to Questhaven's state senator confirmed this fact and a copy of the proposed legislation was in the mail. On receipt of the Assembly bill, it turned out to be a cleverly worded reversal of Questhaven's victory in the California Superior Courts. Mr. K was on the threshold of gaining as a lawmaker what had eluded him as a lawyer. Not only had he introduced the bill itself, but it had passed unopposed through the State Assembly and was now in the Senate's Revenue and Taxation Committee enroute to unopposed passage into law.

Stephen Isaac and their lawyer flew to Sacramento on the day the bill was scheduled to be presented in the afternoon hearing of the Senate committee. They spent the morning meeting with each of the committee members, apprising them of the duplicity behind Assemblyman K's innocent appearing bill. When the committee convened, Mr. K, in an unruffled manner presented his bill as if it was a reasonable clarification of the law regarding tax exempt property for religious purposes. Then the questioning began. Slowly, it came to light that this piece of legislation was unique to a very narrow set of conditions such that, when asked what properties would be affected by its passage, he didn't think there were too many, henceforth, not a major impact on anyone.

At this point, the chairman of the committee, Senator George Deukmejian who later became California's governer, asked Mr. K if, as an attorney, he had ever lost a case involving the tax exemption of a place in San Diego County named Questhaven Retreat? He admitted that, yes, he had lost such a case. He next was asked to identify any other property in the state that would be affected by this bill. Mr. K answered that he could not, whereupon Senator Deukmejian, his voice heavy in rebuke, said that there was no more disreputable act for a lawmaker to perpetrate than to pass a law that reversed a court decision such a lawmaker lost as a former attorney. With that, the committee terminated the bill and Mr. K quietly slipped out of the room. It was indeed a moment of truth.

The years passed and the Ministry carefully followed the introduction of new legislation in the State Assembly, but no further bills came along related to Questhaven. There was, however, one final ominous development. Mr. K was eventually appointed as a judge in the Superior Court system of San Diego County by another governor with whom he had worked closely while an Assemblyman. This meant the Ministry's attorney was instructed, in the event of any future litigation, to reserve its right of challenge for Mr. K exclusively. Happily, no further contact with him became necessary and the tax-exemption episode concluded with Mr. K's retirement from the bench a few years later.

The entire series of events brought home to Flower the fact that, in all matters involving the light, the Path is not made easy, rather it is made to open the eyes of those responsible for the Retreat, to stretch their reach, and strengthen their resolve. This is particularly true where opposition to the light is concerned. It is for those in charge to learn the art of seeing what needs doing to protect Questhaven and the work.

❧ ✳ ❧

The 1970s brought other offerings and inspiration to Flower and Questhaven. First, a long-awaited gift—sought by Lawrence and bearing his spiritual signature: Friendship House, the spacious hospitality hall and center for social gatherings. Its lovely interior Flower had decorated herself and in her own inimitable way: she selected the handsome floor tile, the draperies, and the furniture from colorful samples each separately, matching them in her mind's eye. The drapes were an original idea, sewing together panels of varied pastel hues into a rhythmic pattern of alternating bright vertical bands. As it could only happen for her, everything harmonized perfectly.

Friendship House

And in the center of the open beam ceiling hung sparkling crystal chandeliers—a touch of elegance and faultless beauty.

The second bestowal came in the heart of India at the site of the Taj Mahal. Their guide, having earlier shown them this wonder of the world in daylight, now took them on an unscheduled night visit in the mystic flame of a full moon. She was awe-struck at its unearthly beauty. What shimmered before their eyes was, in reality, the shrine's ethereal vestment. As in the mountains of Switzerland, the inner and outer planes once more mingled imperceptibly, only this time a masterpiece of humanity wrought the miracle. She no longer needed to describe to others the appearance of the etheric world. It shone revealed.

The third gift awaited her return to Questhaven and concerned her heaviest burden—a lagging, reluctant body and an overworked heart precariously balanced on the edge of life by a strict regime of elaborate meditation, a curtailed diet, frequent medical checkups, and prayer. There was yet another factor overshadowing all of these: her indefatigable spirit. Days when she felt ill outnumbered those of feeling up to her duties; when the effort to get out of bed or take a walk seemed beyond her strength; when everything within her body begged for releasement. Somehow she forced herself to her work, never giving in to the great longing simply to drop her weary body and step into the winged world of eternity. Yet in her prayers she never let the fact of her heart condition limit the vision of unobstructed wholeness.

Then during the past several months she began to feel a freedom from this inertia. Even more remarkable, the demands of a fast-paced world tour hadn't left her drained of vitality but strangely refreshed. She kept her next appointment with the heart specialist mildly curious about what changes he might detect. The findings were astounding, beyond his wildest hopes—she was healed! At first, disbelieving the results, he carefully rechecked the electrocardiogram and each of the ancillary tests, but it was all true. The most he had foreseen was the maintenance of her condition without further deterioration, but now he could say her heart was unaccountably normal for one of her age. She should remain on her present schedule, avoiding long hours, most interviews, and any form of stress, and if she did this she could expect to live a long and normal life.

A long and normal life! The doctor's remark hung in her thoughts like the words of a lovely song. Already she had lived more than twenty years past the age of any previous incarnation in a body kept going, in recent years, by little more than faith. And the outlook for the future all at once was clear and unburdened. The work was firmly established, the teaching formulated, the archetype made manifest. Long ago she thought of this moment as the time she would be called back into God's world. Now it seemed these events were but a prologue to what yet would come. Could this be? Were there more secrets in her future, more surprises?

With a bright glow of peace, wondering upon these things, she did what she had always done and went about the duties of the day, making her way down the trail from her home that led through an oak grove to her study. She paused to listen to the birds greeting her from branches overhead and from bushes on both sides of the canyon. Whatever tomorrow held, she would be ready. And for now, what beauty, what joy filled this shining hour!

Chapter 21

Holy Expectancy

Considering the trials already encountered, from the wildfire of 1943 to the series of tax-exemption engagements over Questhaven's land use beginning in 1967, the Retreat had won a hard-fought and respected reputation for protecting its right to existence in the County of San Diego. When people inquired why it was necessary to endure so many confrontations for a work consecrated to the Lord Christ, Flower answered that wherever the Light is upheld, darkness inevitably puts it to the test of wills. If those supporting the Light persevere, not only will they prevail but in that accomplishment they gain valuable experience in defending the Light in future encounters.

There were other developments of a more welcome nature. In the early 1980s Flower received an inquiry from a young West German publisher for permission to publish one of her books in the German language. She couldn't have been more pleased. It happened that Dr. Peter Michel, founder of the Aquamarin Verlag publishing house located in the Munich area and specializing in esoteric literature was browsing through a book shop one day and came upon an English edition of The Sacred Heart of Christmas. Peter was charmed by the book's style and the quality of its revelations. He committed himself soon thereafter to introduce the book and its author to the German speaking world. With Flower's enthusiastic approval, this became the beginning of an enduring relationship that eventually would see most of her writings translated and made available in German.

Along with the appearance of her books to these eager seekers was an invitation to conduct workshops in Europe. While Flower lacked the stamina to make such a commitment herself, arrangements were made for her associate and his wife to go in her place. This began an exchange of visits back and forth between Europe and Questhaven that continues to this day.

Travelling without the demand to lecture and conduct training sessions still was a delight for Flower. She visited Australia and New Zealand in 1978. Of all the places that journey offered, the discovery of Mt. Cook on the South Island of New Zealand was unforgettable. Here in the midst of an unspoiled wilderness, she found an extraordinary nature presence, Lord Taklaw, who presided over the mountain peak itself and all that it surrounds. What was distinctive about this noble being was his detachment, on the one hand, and his high levels of expectation toward all human visitors, on the other. She immediately sensed his disciplined manner that communicated the importance of shedding all irreverent and superficial attitudes and coming into a surrendered appreciation of the purity and wonder that this initiatory mountain presence offered. One could not find a finer setting for reconsecration and spiritual renewal.

Flower A. Newhouse before Mt. Cook in 1978

For Flower, the value of a spiritual journey into new and unfamiliar places, was the transforming energy such experiences brought forth. There was an openness activated by the fresh vistas and viewpoints streaming into one's consciousness. There was more. She beheld in the nature of travel, a host of opportunities for new beginnings. Take for example a set of rules she composed for another Questhaven group on their way to New Zealand in 1981:

Dear Ones,

The theme for your journey is Holy Expectancy. Around the bend of each hour, every walk, and every event is something precious. Watch for it. Capture it. Look for the golden moment — the exquisite enjoyment — the perfect attunement.

Cherish every person and every event. Sit with different persons at every meal. Get to know everyone. Help all. Remember the Protective Presence.

Lovingly, Flower

The members of that group conscientiously put these rules into practice and the journey was memorable and transforming, in life-changing ways. Those rules became the standard set of instructions for all subsequent spiritual journeys at Questhaven.

Toward the middle to late 1980s Flower health began to show signs of slowing down. By this time she found it difficult to prepare Sunday talks and for awhile she gave question and answer services. But the time soon came that even this was too taxing. She continued giving the invocation on many Sunday mornings, then found it necessary to retire entirely from all such activities. Her last appearance on the speaker's podium was the ordination of two ministers on August 15, 1990, which was the fortieth anniversary of the coming of the Masters in 1950. It was a service that she performed flawlessly and without her reading glasses.

At this time there was a preliminary diagnosis by two physicians that suggested she might be in the early stages of Alzheimers disease. She was now 81 years old, having lived over twice the length of any previous incarnation. It was not surprising that her body was no longer able to keep pace with her spirit. As for the Alzheimers, when she learned of this medical diagnosis she said, "Well, then I will just have to overcome it, won't I." In the eyes of several people who were with her on a regular basis, she did just that. One couple who took her out to lunch on a weekly basis, year after year, never once observed any of the classic signs of this malady: disorientation, bizarre episodes of behavior, profound memory loss, or inappropriate emotional outbursts. She did become quieter, though still able to carry a meaningful conversation, and at times would evince amazing wisdom with respect to a particular situation.

During the summer of 1992 Peter Michel and a group of German and Swiss visitors arrived at Questhaven to film a documentary of Questhaven and Flower's life work. Anticipating that any participation by Flower herself would prove stressful, there was a clear understanding that she might not be able to take part. She was 83 and her health was unpredictable. Yet when the moment of filming arrived, to everyone's amazement and delight, here came Flower into Friendship House. She smiled, greeting everyone, and took a chair in the circle of about twenty visitors. After some opening comments, she invited questions from the gathering. It was one of those magical moments and it soon became obvious that the individual most pleased with the proceedings was Flower herself. It was her farewell appearance to visitors at the Retreat and she conducted herself reminiscent of the Flower of earlier years.

Years earlier, she had made the comment that to have waited on her mission until she had a healthy strong body would have required two additional incarnations. Clearly, it was not in her nature to spare herself this physical luxury at the expense of postponing the work that was so sorely needed in support of humanity's evolution. She was uniquely qualified to bring through the message on Christian mysticism and the Kingdom of the Angels and the time was *now*.

On the morning of July 8, 1994 at her Questhaven home, Flower peacefully made her transition. There was no doubt about the joy and freedom found in her return to her homeland. So often she had described the ecstasy one experiences in rediscovering the inner worlds. And on the shores of Eternity to welcome her home, were her beloved Lawrence and row upon row of her pupils. Her sponsors would say of her, "Well done, thou good and faithful servant."

.

Chapter 22

A Final Trial by Air and Fire

B efore the story of Flower concludes, there remain two more extraordinary challenges to Questhaven Retreat. The first occurred while she was still with us, although no longer active. It completed the trials by the four elements. It began in the form of the placement of a landfill about a half-mile from Questhaven's western boundary. This seemed innocent enough at the time and in the spirit of good citizenship it wasn't protested. Its lifespan was set for fifteen years and then it would become a park or permanent open space. As the fifteen years were winding down, local governments suddenly faced what appeared to be a waste disposal crisis. Attempts to site new landfills were strongly resisted because of their proximity to residential communities or their threat to contaminating ground water. This meant that existing landfills would need to remain in service longer.

What next occurred was unthinkable to the Retreat. A plan was presented to add a trash incineration plant to the existing landfill. As the effects of this proposal sank in, it became clear that in addition to extending the life of this landfill for fifty or more years, it would spew out a steady stream of toxic smoke. Since the Retreat was downwind from this monstrosity, it would bear the principal burden of the plant's air pollution impact.

Researching the track record of such "state of the art" facilities elsewhere in the country, it soon became evident that it was an expensive and troubled technology with more problems than solutions. But to fight it, the path divided into three lines of attack. The first was the technology, proving that it was, in fact, costly, unreliable, and a dangerous source of air pollution. Defending this technology was a battery of so-called experts from the northeastern region of the country, well financed and resourceful. The second line of attack was political—appearing and testifying before city councils, the County Board of Supervisors, and state agencies. And third was legal. To this end the Retreat engaged an excellent attorney to lead the court battle to stop the proposed plant on environmental grounds.

What most threatened the Retreat was the pollution of its air—a pall of smoke, laden with toxic elements, overlying its pristine chaparral-covered hills and oak-lined canyons. The very uniqueness that distinguished Questhaven as a place in nature that promised an inspiring and healthy setting would now be so seriously compromised that it would no longer be able to attract visitors.

Thus began a confrontation that was to last over six years and involve a number of lawsuits. While Questhaven's attorney was not successful in every case, one of his earlier filings, on appeal, forced a delay in the efforts to begin construction of the incinerator plant that turned out to be crucial. It was during this delay that a shift in the vote of one of the county supervisors was sufficient to cancel support of the project. Had the attorney failed to successfully argue a reversal of judgement in the Appellate Court, the plant would have become a reality along with its miserable outflow of pollution.

An interesting observation presented itself about this time. It was noticed that in the unfolding history of the Retreat, a curious pattern had emerged involving the four basic elements. It began with the trial by fire in 1943. Second was the trial by earth in 1953 brought about by the trespassing incident to establish a hostile right-of-way across the heart of its property. Third, the fight to establish its own water district in

1958. And finally, to preserve the Retreat's air quality beginning in 1984. Nor was the pattern exhausted. Also involving the earth was the Retreat's series of battles to establish the tax exception of its land. And, as history would have it following Flower's transition, there was yet another encounter with fire.

Regarding these trials, Flower was never fearful or pessimistic regarding Questhaven's future. She kept the faith of the Great Ones whose choice this property was with the realization that all would be well as long as those in charge remained vigilant, taking nothing for granted. In these matters, she followed a practical rule—prepare for the worst but expect and visualize the best. Regarding the future, one of the trusted attorneys who had served the Retreat's legal needs over the years foresaw that the most obvious prize Questhaven posed in the eyes of a materialistic world was its land. Whether this took the form of encroaching developments on its boundaries, the penetration of major highways by force of the eminent domain powers of city and county governments, or unwelcome industrial activity, the risk would always be a factor to reckon with.

❧ ✳ ❧

As the twentieth century drew to a close, there remained Questhaven's most fateful encounter of all. One of Questhaven's outstanding natural assets was its magnificent stand of chaparral, much of which remained untouched by fire for over a hundred years. Reaching up as high as twelve to fifteen feet, and nearly impenetrable, it was classified by botanists as one of San Diego County's finest surviving stands of chaparral. On the downside, given its age and density, was an enormous quantity of deadwood that was an explosive source of fuel for some future fire.

What everyone feared, fire fighters most of all, was the

situation when dry winds off the desert known as Santa Anas might combine with a source of ignition to create a fire storm: wild, swirling, erratic flames engulfing everything in their path and advancing at speeds up to fifty miles per hour.

October 21, 1996, began much like any other day in the fall of the year. The weather was clear with a forecast of Santa Ana winds off the desert blowing in gusts. By early afternoon there were reports of fires elsewhere in San Diego County such that the sky was hazy with drifting clouds of smoke. Coming home from a morning of errands and shopping, the director and his wife walked up the hill above their home to the Retreat's reservoir, seeking the best view of the surrounding countryside. There were no signs of any fire activity in their vicinity and they returned to their home somewhat relieved. Still, there was a heaviness to the atmosphere and about a half-hour later, the director returned to the reservoir for another scan of the horizon. Joined by two co-workers, they studied the horizon for any signs of dense smoke rising rapidly into the sky that would indicate a fire close by. Then suddenly off to the east a thin dark column of smoke rose up like the funnel of a dust devil perhaps three or four miles distant. This was the worst of all possible positions for a fire front driven by the desert winds heading straight for Questhaven.

Quickly, the decision to evacuate the Retreat was made and everyone dispersed to rescue what could be saved. Still, in everyone's minds the fire was perhaps an hour away so there was no panic. Returning to his home the director made some hasty phone calls and, before loading their van with valuables, quickly made his way for one last assessment of the advancing fire. What met his eyes upon reaching the reservoir was unbelievable. The eastern horizon was a wall of flames. The winds had picked up and were later clocked at about thirty-five miles per hour with gusts close to fifty. There was no time to save anything at home with the exception of gathering together their cat and two dogs before racing to the Church of the Holy Quest and rescuing two of its most treasured portraits.

Passing in front of its stained glass windows which faced the fire front now descending upon the church itself, the director and his wife found the heat was so intense it seemed certain that the stained glass panels were about to implode. The two portraits were removed and quickly they reached their van and withdrew to the parking lot. By this time the first of the fire trucks was arriving. The air was a spectacle of flying cinders blown by the hot wind a hundred or more yards in advance of the fire front itself. Classified later as a true fire storm, the flames swirled in chaotic fashion, sending firebrands in all directions making it impossible to protect anything except human life. All the while the fire leapt in giant strides westward through the Retreat and on toward the Pacific Ocean.

On their way out, the director and his wife, upon reaching a roadside vantage point, took one last look across the valley to the smoke-engulfed Retreat. At that moment, there was every indication that Questhaven was a total loss, so consuming were the flames and so dark and dense the boiling cauldron of smoke.

No one was allowed to return until the next day, although it turned out that two of the Retreat's co-workers courageously remained on the grounds throughout the fire and performed what protection they could all night long. Coming up the road to the Retreat's entrance was like entering upon a moonscape. Not a sprig of green remained and the entire landscape was a barren wasteland. It was heartbreaking. Approaching Questhaven, however, there was a hopeful sign. The evergreens that formed Questhaven's parklike central area had somehow survived. To everyone's amazement all of the buildings used for retreat activities were untouched by the fire: the office, Friendship House, all guest facilities, and miracle of miracles, the Church of the Holy Quest. At the very forefront of the advancing fire, squarely in its path, there was not so much as a scorch mark visible. The only damage due to intense heat was a number of tiny cracks in the stained glass windows. When the fire chief inspected the church afterward, he couldn't explain its survival. By all accounts it should have been the first building consumed.

The Retreat did lose three homes including that of the founders, with extensive damage to two others, as well as the Retreat's enclosed reservoir. But considering the nature of the firestorm that struck the Retreat that day, it was an extraordinary outcome. One neighbor nearby owning property with several homes lost everything. Altogether, 130 homes were destroyed by the fire as it continued to the coast. It was the most destructive fire in the County's history.

As time passed and insurance settlements began to repair the damage, benefits of the fire began to accumulate. Perhaps its most noteworthy accomplishment was the cleaning out of a century or more of accumulated deadwood in the chaparral that blanketed the hills—a necessary cleansing that sooner or later must take place. It is also nature's way of rejuvenating this botanical complex known as the elfin forest.

Homes were repaired or rebuilt, bringing them up to current building codes. But the jewel emerging from this furnace of adversity was the Retreat's Academy and Library Building erected on the site of the founders' home.

Containing the living quarters for a resident minister, this handsome facility enjoys a view that is breathtaking. It also became the garden center of Questhaven with inviting benches for individual reflection or outdoor gatherings. The most valued feature of this location, however, was the consecrated energies that the founders themselves left imprinted in the foundation of this Academy building. For all the many uses it will serve, it will forever be a shrine to those two courageous faith-filled pioneers who rekindled the flames of Christian mysticism illuminating for all who follow in their footsteps, the new millennium.

In the passage of time, these holy grounds that consti-tute Questhaven Retreat will stand out as a spiritual sanctu-ary and nature preserve without equal. Its founders will be remembered as far-seeing mystics who grounded a unique vision tapping the wellsprings of Christianity's future—a fu-ture that opens the gates of humanity's consciousness to the Kingdom of God that lies within each of us.

Epilogue

The story of Flower and the work she and her husband Lawrence founded doesn't end here. She left a legacy of teachings that rekindle the flames of Christian mysticism. She has described the Angel Kingdom more authentically, revealing its true nature, than any other author—their appearance, their many orders, their evolutionary pathways and their works. But her dominant focus as a teacher was ever the awakening of humanity to the joy, the art, and the love of living the life and following the way of the Living Christ. In her eyes, that was the alpha and the omega of what life on the planet earth is about. As she often explained to her many pupils, she was judged as a teacher by the Higher Ones in terms of the lives she awakened and set afire spiritually, bringing about their transformation.

She left another legacy that generations to come will richly share—Questhaven Retreat and its 655 acres of pristine nature wilderness forming a hill-hidden island of tranquility in northern San Diego County. Questhaven is Flower and Lawrence, or more exactly, it is the gift of their lives summed up in peerless exampleship. Every acre, every victory, every truth that defines Questhaven will have been sanctified by their integrity to the quest that is both timeless and boundless. Questhaven truly is an outpost on the shores of eternity, fulfilling its mission as a link between humanity and the Christ consciousness. It is a wisdom school, a way of life summoning those who long have searched for a path to God that hews to the Christ, the Christ who is universal, who is Lord of All

Religions on the Earth.

The way is simple, as all great truths are simple. Foremost among its qualities is love. She once said of herself: "The strange thing about my temperament is the peculiar love I have which nearly tears me apart sometimes. (Tears filled her eyes as she described this.) But I love nature so, and beauty. It's a highly emotional feeling for me; its roots go down so very deep. It's like the love of the Christ. I tune in on His vibration and the way He sees life. I turn His attitude upon animals and people. I can be more detached toward people, but with animals and nature I have no way of being impersonal. I will love a tree as much as an animal. (Now she laughed with delight.) When I would express this kind of love to Lawrence, he was always very responsive but it puzzled him. He said to a friend before he died he wished he could have loved more deeply himself."

About her there was a great presence of love, an outflow of caring for others that loved the total, passing beyond the surface of the individual, sinking into his soul. And when the soul of this person responded, she held her love for them up to that level constantly. That's why she was closest of all to nature and to animals; people, having egos, put up barriers. Because of this, she frequently reminded her audiences, "The Higher Ones never praise a disciple." This was also her rule as a teacher, balancing firmness with an all-encompassing love. She wanted others to see themselves as she could see them—from the highlands of their soul. Once that happened they would never again be satisfied with themselves at a lower level.

The quality of purity follows love. Her own words again tell it best: "You are charged always by your guardian to think constructively of others and to keep your vessel pure and self-emptied. Thus, what reaches others is pure. This is really hard to do sometimes. When I am most enthusiastic about a lecture

I have a great struggle to become self-emptied and I am tested by the thought that *I can do it myself*.

"My guardian gets after me for little things that wouldn't mean much to others. For instance, because I have had so much training in dancing and singing in other lifetimes, it is very hard for me not to show others my way of doing it. In another situation, during a lecture there was a certain person in the audience who had a severely critical attitude and was doing nothing to change it. I used an example with her need in mind, emphasizing the destructiveness of such a habit. When I finished my talk and sat down, my guardian came to me and, standing directly in front of me, said: 'Can you not teach without scolding?' "

Her appreciation of purity showed up in her tastes in art and music. She lived the words of Keats, "Beauty is truth, truth beauty." Art that exalts humanity's highest moments or richest experiences she adored. Music that lifts one into new states of consciousness won her instant recognition. But when, in the name of realism, art portrays ugliness, sensuality, or chaos as the reflection of our times and music descends to dissonance or raucous orgies of sound and lyrics, she was instantly repulsed. "If people could see clairvoyantly what effects these lower expressions have on the astral body, they would be courting insanity." It puzzled her how people, who would never think of gulping down garbage or wallowing in filth, let their higher bodies suffer just these comparable abuses.

If love and purity symbolize all that is Christ-like in character—and the many other facets of this diamond lie waiting the Aquarian explorer in the treasure caves of her writings—then the one remaining, outshining quality encompassed Flower's reality: her unique clairvoyance. Over the years, numerous individuals with degrees of this unfoldment have come to Questhaven. None possessed anything approaching

251

Flower's incomparable oneness with the inner worlds. Some proved to be unstable individuals indiscriminately experiencing the lower regions of the astral plane, projecting into these transient apparitions their longing to contact great personages and happenings. The rest only caught clouded fragments and lacked her memory's continuity over lifetimes allowing the accurate interpretation of these experiences.

The distinctive feature of her genius was her awareness of superphysical emanations, presences, and realities. Her life's joy was to be an instrument that opens the doors of the inner dimensions to anyone who came in touch with her—never for the perilous deflections of phenomena or glamour, but for what happens to the individual when his higher senses begin to stir. Listen to her invitation: "Think of what it is like to walk in nature and see trees as they *really are*, extending twice their physical size in lovely sheaths of light endlessly moving and nourishing the tree's etheric life; to see streams of color, many unknown to man, weaving in and out of forests—hues that are alive, moving like iridescent spirals of mist caught in bank after bank of brightly colored lights.

"Think of what it is like to attend a concert and see luminous musical forms and waves of breath-taking color rising from the orchestra; to recognize music not by melodies or strains alone but by themes of form and color blended into a choreography of moving radiations. Then, to visit an art gallery and see the aura of each painting reaching out into the room; and the painting itself extending alive just as the artist beheld the scene or person at the time: trees moving in the wind and faces changing their expression slightly, richly enhancing their appearance.

"And think what it would be like to sense glorious fragrances no one else notices; to see at unexpected moments presences, archetypes and thought forms that overshadow all life unceasingly: to be able to discover great beauty in some-

EPILOGUE

one whose outer appearance is quite plain; to see the nobility of character and sincerity shining out from here or there in a crowd of people—even to know when someone is exaggerating or not telling the truth by the gray-brown tints in his aura.

"As a counselor, envision what it would be like to study a person's aura to notice what colors are dominant, indicating his mood or temperament; to observe whether the aura is a contracted oval, as with the average person, or an expanded one when the individual is more advanced. Imagine looking for symbols and archetypes in the aura that would have been implanted there by the Higher Intelligences signifying important keynotes to which this person is spiritually committed; and to distinguish these from ordinary thought forms because the former glisten and vibrate, broadcasting an unbroken signal to the recipient.

"On a Sunday morning, picture using clairvoyance to examine the audience to detect who is weary or burdened, expectant or eager; to observe the Angelic visitors above the audience, mantling the service, and what different orders are represented.

"Then, again in nature, to travel to a national park or lovely forest region to study the supervising nature intelligences and the color bands in the auras of the mountains, grasping their significance; to behold on the peaks themselves a great Allray or an Allsee, two of the highest orders of nature Angels, and from whom flow rivers of wondrous color circulating down into the aura of the mountain itself.

"And in the mountains at night, can you imagine taking a walk and seeing the trees radiating a silver sheen tinted toward tones of white or turquoise depending on the species; and then to realize this sparkling silver quality appears only at night because the nature servers change shifts at sunset. While the daylight beings go to a nature playground for their renewal, the night beings undertake another work which generates this distinctive emanation."

She once commented about what she sees at the Christmas season. Driving by some residences she pointed out how, on the inner, most of the decorative lights had little spiritual radiance but, here and there, were shining exceptions. She then explained that these had been hung with the love of preparation in honor of the Christ's nativity. And gifts have the same uneven appearance clairvoyantly. Those that are purchased and wrapped routinely, no matter their cost, have no special glow about them, but those that are prepared selflessly for the joy of giving seem on fire with light.

Sleep, for everyone, is the time of renewal for the inner bodies. The difference is that Flower remembered these experiences upon awakening. While her physical form rested, she stepped out into the vast reaches of the inner worlds, sometimes to work with pupils under her direction and other times to visit favorite centers of instruction or refreshment. In the higher dimensions she described numerous spiritual cities. The City of St. Stephen, the City of St. John, and Shamballa, the seat of the earth's Inner Government, are the three she most often frequented. From her travels, she became acquainted with power centers above Lake Patzcuaro and Mt. Popocatepetl, Mexico, Machu Picchu in Peru and most recently, the vicinity overshadowing the Taj Mahal in India. There is also a certain mountain near Questhaven where several great nature Angels reside and she frequently went there for its unusual recharging.

Once, when asked if she were a medium, she answered, "No. Mediums let themselves be used by other spirits. I am clairvoyant and all that I do is done consciously and for the spiritual advancement, never the curiosity, of the person involved." She used her clairvoyance to continually investigate the world situation and the needs and growth levels of individuals.

One final word about Flower's clairvoyance is essential. It was a gift she attained gradually under the close supervision of many teachers and requiring lifetimes of preparation and purification, culminating in her incarnation with Pythagoras. The young student is grossly unrealistic to expect it sooner for himself. Unfortunately, his keen wish for this prize can arouse unconscious forces within his personality self capable of simulating such contacts, much as dreams are created during sleep. These projections from the unconsciousness, mistaken for authentic receptions, reinforce his ego's desire to "be somebody spiritually" and a flood of counterfeit experiences follow. Coupled with this deflection is the simultaneous possibility that the individual actually will contact regions of the lower astral plane which the ambitious expectations of his ego seize upon as the highest pinnacles of the inner worlds. Flower's charter for the training program at Questhaven aims directly at this pitfall by giving first priority to the disciplines of preparation.

Paralleling her clairvoyance was a second gift of equal merit though easily obscured by its more subtle nature: *intuition*. This was the genius of Pythagoras and the art he passed on to all of his pupils. It forms the gateway to enlightenment by imprinting upon consciousness impressions and realizations from the ceaseless currents of Divinity: when the channel is purified of self, its receptions are altogether as trustworthy and far-reaching as superphysical perception. Though Flower's clairvoyance commanded the most attention and wonder, it was her intuition that most often guided her in making decisions, sensing needs, anticipating problems, and turning toward new undertakings. In training those who will someday take her place, who will need to be responsive to the directions of the Hierarchy overshadowing the world, it is this gateway she watched and cultivated.

Above all else, Flower was a *wayshower*, finding in everything the possibilities of enlightenment and growth. The training program at Questhaven, though centered around the lessons spoken weekly from the lectern or printed from time to time in various publications, depends in the end upon application—it must manifest in the aspirant's choices, motivations, and actions. Her concern focused on the pupil's personality self—is it being surrendered? Her expectation, on the other hand, was for evidence of a pupil's teachableness, his willingness to go all the way under direction. Once this quality appeared, growth followed rapidly.

About those with strong egos who quickly expect to become teachers themselves she once observed, "Too many mistake the call to preparation for the call to service." Yet she approached each person with the faith that they could overcome their obstacles without delay. It is, after all, up to them and until they are stopped by self-imposed limitations she offered every encouragement, inviting forth their highest effort.

With the personality self she was unyielding, never feeding it with flattery or smoothing over its ruffled feathers. For the real individuality to emerge, the lesser self must die! This, the crucifixion experience, is the mountain she climbed, and all who aspire to follow the way of the Christ must face the same ascent.

Though she supported the teachings of metaphysics, its tendency to glorify the mind and its entrenched resident, the ego—rather than the service of God—has caused problems particularly with people wanting the mystical outlook of Questhaven without letting go of their need for an inflated self-esteem often unwittingly reinforced in metaphysics. No one drew close to her who was not required to make this choice just as she had to make it. It was not a choice the majority of metaphysical students expect or welcome and for the many who were attracted by her clairvoyance, few were prepared to enter into the discipline behind it. Yet as she was, she taught. This was her way and whether it becomes the way of tens or hundreds or thousands always will hinge on the question of self-surrender.

In the interest of expanding her work, she was frequently urged to relocate in Hollywood or closer to larger cities rather than center her work at a retreat in a remote rural area. Questhaven is not easily found, lying off the main thoroughfares, and many people are unprepared for its simple cottages and vastness of nature. A prominent lecturer and international news correspondent from Los Angeles once spent the night in one of these cottages before addressing the congregation on Sunday morning. In his opening remarks the next day, he said never in his life had he been engulfed in such a silence. In the midst of a hectic routine rushing him along noisy freeways to distant battlefields, then to be swallowed up unexpectedly in the peace of such a place made an impression upon him he would cherish forever. One observation of this rank from a person weary of the city's pace and the world's burdens, answers a thousand inquiries by others who saw in Flower the makings of a celebrity, given the support of the "right people in the right setting."

Beyond these glimpses of Flower, and those shared in the story, so much remains unsaid. Writing of her life and Lawrence's is like being led to a room filled with the crown jewels of a great kingdom, then being asked to select from its thousands of treasures the one hundred most beautiful objects. The mind boggles at the task, and it is the intuition that must sort through the dazzling array.

Yet even of these things known of her life and experience, what remains altogether hers, unspoken, is the far greater share. She recently expressed it this way: "Ninety-nine percent of what I receive from the inner side of life, I never reveal to anyone"—a staggering disclosure.

Among the remaining one percent are her prayers during

257

services; all spontaneous and unrehearsed just as she trained her pupils always to pray, that the Spirit may speak. Each one was a unique baptism of light and would never again pass from her lips. They were beyond recapture since they included her presence before one, the chapel filled with hushed people, and the power that only comes at such a moment. Yet the words survive in the tape recordings made of each service over the years.

On a Sunday in August, 1968, she gave such a benediction blessing. With its words—her words, trailing off as they always do into the future of ourselves—this writing ends:

A sensitive who has character and who has achieved permeability is like a Stradivarius violin—highly tuned, very delicately sensitive, but what melodies of enrichment and mellowness come forth from that instrument. Let us guard the instrumentality of our beings and keep them as violins to be used in the temple, worthy of music unto the Lord.

We have this treasure in earthen vessels,
that the excellency of the power may be of God
and not of ourselves.

II *Corinthians* 4:7

Made in the
USA
Columbia, SC